I0521205

HOW OLD ARE YOU TODAY?

Dementia,
A Mother, A Daughter, and The
Game That Transformed Their Lives

GLENNA HECHT

Copyright © 2025 Glenna Hecht

All rights reserved. No part of this publication may be reproduced, stored in a retrieval system, or transmitted in any form or by any means—electronic, mechanical, photocopying, recording, or otherwise—without the prior written permission of the publisher, except in the case of brief quotations used in reviews or scholarly works.

Published by Hecht Publishing, a division of Humanistic Consulting

This book is available in both print and digital formats.

For inquiries or permissions, contact:

press@howoldareyoutoday.com

ISBN: 979-8-9997871-1-8

First Edition

Disclaimer

This book is meant to offer support, inspiration, and ideas based on personal experience and research. It is not intended as medical, legal, or psychological advice. Every dementia journey is unique, and readers are encouraged to consult with qualified healthcare professionals for guidance tailored to their specific needs.

The author and publisher are not responsible for any outcomes related to the use of the information or game shared in this book.

Dedication

To all caregivers—you are true heroes.

Whether you're supporting loved ones or answering a professional calling, your compassion, resilience, and tireless care make a profound difference in the lives of others. This book is for you—a source of hope and connection during the difficult and often heartbreaking journey of dementia.

To my parents—thank you for teaching me to dream boldly and believe I could make a difference. This book is a testament to you, to our love, and to the life we shared.

Table of Contents

Introduction
How Old Are You Today?

You're a caregiver. But this isn't the life you planned. It feels like someone else's story—one you never asked for.

Your days blur together: doctor's appointments, medications, repetitive questions, and the heartbreak of seeing someone you love lose pieces of themselves.

Maybe you're desperate, hoping for a moment of peace—or even joy—somewhere in all this. You wonder: Is that even possible?

Because dementia is supposed to be cruel—a slow, relentless goodbye.

But what if it doesn't have to be that way?

What if dementia isn't just a long fading—but a chance to say something truly meaningful?
A way to connect, to remember, to laugh—even when reality has shifted?

This book is a dementia love story—built on a game, lived with heart.

It's the story of how I—an only child—who took a job across the country to get away from my mother—ended up spending nine years caring for her.

I moved her five times: from Chicago to Dallas, through assisted living, memory care, and ultimately, a nursing home when the money ran out.

I tried everything to fix her: certifications, research, seminars and support groups.

Nothing worked.

Then I stumbled onto a simple question game.
It became our lifeline.
It became a way to time-travel into her past—a way to meet her where she was.
It was the key that unlocked peace, joy, and a bond I never thought possible.

That game added life to her final years—and it gave me a second chance to show up with love, patience, and presence.

This book is the result—and the gift—of that discovery. It's packed with stories—about me and my mom—but they could just as easily be about your dad, your aunt, or whoever you're walking this path with.

And it's also a guide: how you can use this question game to unlock hidden worlds, give yourself hope, create peace, and yes—even find joy, in the darkest rooms of dementia.

Because using dementia to reconnect isn't just possible.
It's beautiful.
And it can be your story, too.

Chapter 1
Mom Is Missing

When we look back on our lives, certain moments burn themselves into memory—snapshots so profound, they change everything. Some moments, you can prepare for—weddings, the birth of a child, crossing the finish line of a marathon. Others blindside you—the news of an illness, a sudden job loss, a phone call that changes everything.

Monday, July 2, 2007—It was just another Monday. Until it wasn't.

My coffee was cold, my inbox overflowing, and I was already debating whether I had time for lunch. Then, the phone rang. My cousin's voice cut through my routine like a blade.

"Your Mom is missing. She ran out of her apartment this morning and didn't come back. The police have been called. You need to come home as soon as possible."

I froze. For a moment, all I could do was nod, as if she could see me through the phone.

"Okay," I whispered, though nothing about this was okay.

The words felt automatic—like my brain was buffering, trying to catch up to the reality of what I had just heard.

Missing.

"Okay," I whispered. The word felt automatic, like my brain was stalling—grasping for control while the ground shifted beneath me. I promised to call back and hung up.

Mom was in her 80s. She didn't have a cell phone. I had no way to reach her. No way to know if she was safe. I hated that feeling more than anything. I called the police, but they hadn't found her.

Then it hit.

Missing. Alone. Wandering the streets of Chicago. What if she's hurt?

What if they can't find her?

What if I'm already too late?

Anything could happen.

What would happen if I left?

I had so many commitments, people relying on me. But as quickly as those thoughts arrived, they vanished.

I only had one mom.

I had to go.

I walked straight into my boss's office. My voice was calm, but inside, I was unraveling.

"My Mom is missing. She's wandering around the city of Chicago, and I need to leave tomorrow. I don't know how long I'll be gone. If you need to replace me, I understand—but I must go."

He didn't hesitate. "Go. Take as long as you need."

I nodded, thanked him, and walked out of the building —unsure when, or if, I'd be back.

I made it to the parking lot. Barely.

Chapter 2
Fear and Realization

The moment I got to my car, the gravity of it all hit me. I sat behind the wheel, unable to move. My hands were trembling. My feet felt like concrete blocks pressed into the floorboard. I wasn't sure I could even lift them to press the pedals.

I couldn't breathe.

What if I didn't make it in time? What if I never saw her alive again?

I checked my phone again. No missed calls. No texts. The silence was unbearable.

And then—guilt.

Our relationship had been strained for years by arguments, hurtful words, and emotional walls built to protect us both. I had convinced myself that distance was necessary, that leaving Chicago was the only way to escape the weight of our broken connection. Living without her seemed possible. Keeping my heart armored felt safer.

But now, staring down the possibility of losing her forever, I wasn't thinking about the fights. The distance. The walls I built.

I was thinking about the time I wasted.

As her only child, it didn't matter how complicated things had become. I was the one who had to show up. I needed to pull myself together.

So, I did what I've always done when overwhelmed: I made a list, one step at a time.

Step 1: Turn the key in the ignition.
Step 2: Look in the mirror.
Step 3: Back out carefully.
Step 4: Drive home safely.

Simple. Doable. The only way I could keep moving

When I got home, another list began forming:

- Book a flight.
- Pack a bag.
- Call family and relay plans.
- Eat ice cream, it will make you feel better.
- Try to get some sleep.

A few minutes before 8:00pm, the phone rang. I snatched it before it rang twice.

It was the doorman from the building. "Your mother is safe. She wandered through the front door as though nothing had happened. She went upstairs to her apartment. I knocked on her door to check on her, and she seemed fine."

Relief hit. Hard.

But even as I exhaled, I knew this wasn't over. The knots in my stomach wouldn't loosen.

I wasn't sure I could face what was waiting for me.

Tomorrow, I will go home.

I had been running for years.

Tomorrow, it will catch up to me.

Chapter 3
Running from the Angels

I barely slept.

By morning, I was on a plane to Chicago, then in a rental car, heading to pick up my cousin for strength and moral support.

I needed backup—someone to walk into this with me.

As we headed downtown, I tried to formulate a plan. I was a problem-solver, after all. That's what I did— identify the issue, produce a solution, execute, and move on.

If all went well, I'd check on my mom, stay a few days, and be back in Dallas before the week was out.

That was the plan.

But plans mean nothing when you are dealing with the unpredictable.

We pulled up in front of my mom's high-rise apartment, and there she was, standing on the sidewalk as if she had been waiting for me—or for someone else.

A heavy weight settled in my chest, pressing against my ribs.

Something was wrong.

She wore a navy blue trench coat that dwarfed her, the hem dragging on the ground, the sleeves swallowing her hands. Gold shoes. A gold purse strapped across her chest, clutched tightly as if it held all the secrets of the world.

I got out of the car and walked toward her, unsure of how she would respond.

Then, as she turned to face me, her coat fell open.

I froze.

She wasn't wearing any clothes. Just her underwear.

How long had she been out here like this?

Had anyone helped her?

Had anyone even noticed?

She had always been small, but now she looked like she was disappearing. Wasting away. A hollowed-out version of the woman I had known.

My mother—so proud, so put together—now looked lost and frantic.

While I was living my life, trying to outrun my responsibilities with her, she had been unraveling. And I had let it happen.

I forced a smile. "Hi, Mom."

She looked at me with darting eyes, full of terror. Then she whispered, "The angels are after me, and I'm afraid. Will you save me?"

I swallowed the panic rising in my chest. "Of course."

Her eyes searched for mine, desperate. "Take me to the synagogue. They won't find me there."

The synagogue?

Breathe. Stay calm. Think.

I forced a nod. "OK, Mom. I will take you, but you must do exactly what I say so you'll be safe. Do you promise?"

She nodded.

I quickly walked back to the car, turned to my cousin, and whispered through clenched teeth, "She's losing her mind. She thinks the angels are chasing her and asked me to take her to the synagogue to be safe. I told her that's where we're going, but we're taking her to the hospital. Please help me."

My cousin just stared, wide-eyed, as if she had stepped into a nightmare she wasn't prepared for.

I got out and gently guided my Mom to the back seat.

"Mom, you need to crouch down on the floor and curl into a little ball. That way, you'll be safe."

She did exactly as I asked, tucking herself into the smallest space possible, her face pressed close to the floor, eyes squeezed shut as if disappearing completely would protect her.

I started the car and pulled away from the rescue spot.

During the drive, she kept peeking up, just enough to check if the danger had passed.

"Stay down, Mom," I whispered. "Not yet."

She immediately folded herself back into the floor.

A few minutes later, her head lifted again.

"Just a little longer," I said gently.

I didn't know if I was saying it for her or for myself.

She ducked down once more, silent, motionless.

Ten agonizing minutes later, we pulled into the emergency entrance of the hospital.

I slammed the car into park, sprinted into the emergency room, and yelled: "My mom is in the car, and she thinks she is being followed by angels. Please help me!"

The people in the emergency room reacted quickly. A nurse called for assistance, and an attendant rushed toward me with a wheelchair.

We ran outside.

I flung open the car door.

My mom was still curled up on the floor, her body pressed as close to the seat as possible.

I crouched down next to her. "Mom, it's okay. You can get up now."

She hesitated, scanning the area before stepping out of the car and settling into the wheelchair.

I turned to the attendant, my voice shaking. "I have no idea what's going on. I just need her to come out of this alive."

Inside the waiting room, I guided her to a quiet corner, away from prying eyes.

I leaned in close and whispered, "Stay very still. Don't move. If we're quiet, the angels won't find us."

She nodded, eyes wide, scanning every person in the room, assessing if they were an angel coming for her.

I filled out paperwork, my hands shaking as I scrawled my name.

And then we waited.

And waited.

And waited.

Every serious injury, every heart attack, every trauma case took priority over my little mother in her oversized coat.

Friends came, bringing food we barely touched.
Donuts. Coffee.
Things that felt ridiculous in the face of what was happening.

A nurse appeared with a hospital gown. "She'll need to change before we can admit her."

My Mom recoiled, shaking her head. She said the gown was an angel uniform. Looking at it, I kind of saw it too.

I had to think fast.

My cousin. My friend. My mother. Me.

Four women in hospital gowns.

The people in the emergency room looked at us, trying to figure out what was going on.

I smiled and shrugged.

We didn't know what was going on either.

When the nurse came to wheel her away, she looked from one to another, trying to determine who the patient was.

I pointed to my mom. "I'll explain later."

The nurse gave me one last confused look, then wheeled my mother behind the silver doors into the emergency room.

And just like that, she was gone.

The doors shut.

And I waited, not sure what I was waiting for.

Chapter 4
Dementia: That Wasn't Part of the Plan

My skin stuck to the plastic seat cushion. The wooden armrests pressed into my palms as I gripped them like a lifeline.

Waiting.

The minutes dragged; morning bled into afternoon.

Memorize something. Take inventory. Occupy the mind. Do anything to shove down the fear.

- Six chairs.
- Beige industrial carpet, frayed at the entryway.
- Dime-store landscape art in brown plastic frames.
- A window blind with 48 slats.
- Brown-speckled tiles, scuffed from years of pacing.

Every thirty minutes, the receptionist droned the same line in a voice drained of interest: "For now, your mom is having tests completed. We will tell you when she is finished."

"For now?" What does that mean? What about later?

I had noticed the changes—the repeating stories, the odd behavior, the way she seemed to lose time.

But I pushed it aside.

She was aging. She seemed independent. I had convinced myself this was normal.

I wanted to believe everything was fine. Her independence let me keep living my life without worry. Now, there was no denying it, I had ignored the signs I did not want to see.

Hours passed.

A nurse finally appeared at the metal emergency room door and barked out my name.

I stood; we were to follow her.

What was behind those doors?
The answers I had been waiting for.
The answers I was afraid to hear.

The emergency room was chaos—beeping monitors, frantic voices, the sharp scent of antiseptic.

The nurse pulled back a curtain.

The bed was empty.

Panic slammed into my chest.

The nurse saw my face drain of color. "She'll be here in a moment. Have a seat."

So, I sat. My family was with me, and we did not say a word.

Hostage in this curtained room, I did what I had done all day, memorizing my surroundings.

- ◆ Monitors.
- ◆ Bandages.
- ◆ Posters.
- ◆ Cotton swabs.
- ◆ Beige chipped cabinets.

A voice cut through my thoughts. "Your mom is on her way downstairs. She's completed this round of tests."

"This round?" The wording stuck in my head. How many rounds were there?

Mom was wheeled in on a gurney, swaddled in a hospital blanket, the fabric tucked up to her chin.

She looked so small. So fragile. So...old.

We gathered around her.

The doctor stood at the head of the gurney, scanning the faces around him before his eyes landed on me.

The responsible party.

"Your mom appears to be in perfect health. Her vital signs are strong. The infection from the cut on her hand is likely causing some confusion—we've started antibiotics.

"But…"

He paused.

"We believe she may have dementia, and we'll have to run more tests to verify."

I blinked. Dementia?

The word sat in the air, heavy, unfamiliar.

I had no clue what that meant—for her, for me, for anything.

I stared at the doctor, my face blank, waiting for him to say more.

He must have seen the confusion because he softened his tone and continued.

"Dementia isn't just memory loss. It's a condition that affects how the brain works, thinking, reasoning, and eventually, daily function. In the beginning, she may forget things, repeat herself, or lose track of time. But over time, it progresses. People with dementia can forget where they are, who they're with, even who they are. It changes how they process the world."

My brain tried to register the magnitude of his words.

That was more than forgetting names or misplacing keys.

This was forgetting… everything.

I hesitated, then forced out the next question.

"Are you sure?"

His expression didn't change. "Yes, but we need to confirm. She'll have to be transferred to the psychiatric ward for further testing."

I nodded. "Okay." Because what else could I say?

"Then can she go home?"

The doctor shook his head. "No."

"Not now?"

His eyes stayed on mine.

"Not ever."

I looked at my family.

Their faces were etched with exhaustion and something else—
Pity.

I could hear their unspoken thoughts.

"We told you. Someday you would have to stop running and make peace with your Mom."

Someday.

What day was someday?

It was today.

July 3rd.

The day I lost my independence.

Mom stared at me, her big brown eyes wide and uncertain.

She needed me to say something. Anything.

She was scared.

I was scared.

A tear slid down my cheek.

Her long, bony fingers wrapped around mine in a vice grip.

I squeezed her hand. The words that left my mouth changed everything.

"We will get through this together. I will be here for you."

Her eyes filled with tears.

A single drop slid down her cheek, mirroring mine.

She didn't need to speak. I could see it in her eyes.

And just like that, our journey through dementia began.

Dementia wasn't just about forgetting—it was about a world quietly unraveling, piece by piece. I wasn't sure what this meant for her, or for me. But one thing was certain, nothing would ever be the same.

Chapter 5
The Clues Left Behind

I left the hospital, drove to my mom's apartment, then walked for miles.
I needed to process everything, flying to Chicago, fleeing the angels, the emergency room, hearing that my mom might have dementia, and now, the looming psych ward stay.
What next?

That night, finally sitting in my mom's apartment, the remaining energy drained from me like a puddle on the floor.

My body ached—not just from exhaustion, but from something deeper. A weight pressing from the inside out.
My mind repeated a single word: Breathe. Breathe. Breathe.

Once I calmed down, I looked around. The apartment was beautiful, filled with lovely art and elegant furniture.

But beneath the surface? Chaos.
Out-of-date food in the fridge. Half-eaten meals stashed in cabinets, growing mold. Forgotten, waiting for a day that never came.
Stacks of unopened mail. Bills unpaid.

Thirty-six brand-new white shirts, tags still attached. Eighty-six pairs of hosiery, untouched.

The excess, the scattered details—her slipping grasp on daily life was right in front of me. Other memories quickly surfaced, sharper now than before.

I remembered the odd phone calls from the building staff, relaying things my mom had said that didn't quite make sense.

Once, she went to the office convinced that someone had broken into her apartment because half of a cake was missing.
"Mom, did you eat it?" I asked.
She paused, eyes darting like she was searching for an answer, then laughed. "Oh... maybe."

It was just a cake.
But it wasn't just a cake.
It was one of many signs I had overlooked.
Now, there was no more overlooking.

I stared at the unopened mail. I had to deal with this.

I found her checkbooks, and then it hit me. I had no authorization to pay her bills. I wasn't listed on her accounts. No power of attorney. No healthcare directive.

I had asked before—about finances, about paperwork —but she always waved me off.
"I don't want to burden you."
She didn't tell me.

And I didn't press.

Now, there was no choice but to figure it out. Fast.

I searched for any scrap of paper that might reveal her wishes or the whereabouts of financial information. Nothing.

I thought back to the dozens of times I had asked my mom about her finances and what she wanted when the time came.
She always brushed it off.
"We'll cross that bridge when the time comes."
OK, Mom, we have crossed the bridge, and the time has come.

I tried to think logically. Who might know something?

Then I remembered—my mom's best friend had a son who was an attorney. Maybe he could help. Maybe she had told him something she hadn't told me.
I will call him tomorrow.

But right now, I had to try to find answers myself.

I remembered my mom hid things. Maybe the clue was hidden in the last place I'd ever expect.

I tore through her apartment for half the night—every drawer, handbag, and shoebox.
I crawled under her dresser, checked inside coat pockets, lifted her mattress.

I found things she had hidden—birthday cards, money, jewelry, old pieces of half-eaten candy—but no paperwork.

Nothing that gave me the answers I needed.

Finally, exhausted, I collapsed onto the pile of clothes and papers I had pulled from her closet and fell asleep in my clothes.

I had a few hours of quiet before the next thing I wasn't ready for.

Chapter 6
Behind the Metal Door

The next morning, I arrived at the hospital and went straight to the emergency room nurses' station.

"I'm here for my mother," I said.

They told me to sit and wait.

Minutes passed. Then, finally, a nurse approached me.

"Your mom is in a room. We will go and get her together to bring her to the psych ward."

Now I remembered. The doctor had mentioned the psych ward the day before, but I hadn't fully understood what that meant.

"What do you mean, the psych ward?" I asked.

The nurse must have sensed the anxiety in my voice.

"That is where we run the tests to confirm dementia. She will be staying there for the next few days."

We went to my mom's room. She was wearing a hospital gown and looked small, yet safe. I kissed her and told her she was going to another location so they could run further tests.

We rolled her out of her room, into the elevator, and up to another floor.

Then, I saw it.

A metal door. Small round window. Locked.

A buzzer sounded. The door clicked open.

We rolled my mom inside.

At the nurse's desk, a woman sat typing, barely glancing up as we passed.

The reality sank in.

There has to be another way.

If I turn and run away, will anyone notice?

We wheeled her to the front desk.

A nurse stood, looked at my mom, verified her name, and then turned to me.

"She will be here for four days. We will call to let you know how she is doing."

"Can I visit her?"

"Yes."

She continued speaking. "We have assigned visiting hours...."

Her mouth moved, explaining the rules, but I wasn't hearing a word.

My eyes wandered to the other patients in the facility.

It was like a movie.

One man was banging a telephone receiver against the wall, screaming profanity at the top of his lungs.

A woman swayed in her chair to music only she could hear, throwing her hair back and forth like a rock singer.

What had I done?

I turned to the nurse. "Is there an alternative way to diagnose her condition?"

"No. I promise you; she will be alright."

"She is old, in her 80s. She is so little and very scared. I know if this were your mom, you would be fearful for her in these surroundings. Could she possibly stay in a room by herself? She will feel safe."

The nurse nodded.

I leaned over to kiss my mom's cheek, fighting to hold back tears.

"I will come and visit."

A lone tear dripped onto her hand.

Mom tried to calm me. "Don't worry. I am fine."

On the other side of the metal door, I stopped.

Through the small, round window, I saw her—framed in the glass like a portrait.

She was alone and trapped.

She could not leave.

I thought, please protect her. She is my mom. My only mom.

Chapter 7
Seeing Stars

Once Mom settled into the psych ward, I couldn't just sit and wait. I had four days—four days—to find her a new home.

But there was one problem: I had no legal standing. No paperwork. No power of attorney. No right to make decisions on her behalf. And the assisted living facilities made it clear—without the paperwork, I couldn't schedule a tour, reserve a room, or even ask questions.

Before anything else, I had to make a phone call.

I grabbed her "old-school" paper telephone book. The thing was so ancient, the pages were stuffed into the binder like a beat-up paperback. I flipped through, half expecting to find rotary dial instructions, and then— I saw a name.

It belonged to a woman mom always mentioned fondly. And yes—she was the one with "the Jewish attorney son," as mom always described him. Not maliciously. Just a matter of fact, as if it was part of his actual job title. I picked up the phone and dialed.

"Hi, I hope you can help me. My name is Glenna. I believe you are friends with my mom. I found your name in her phone book. She mentioned you often and told me that your son is an attorney. She's currently in the hospital because they believe she has dementia and can no longer live on her own. I'm trying to get some documents in place for her care. I was hoping maybe... he could help."

There was a pause.

Her friend replied, carefully but directly. "I suspected she had dementia. She's said things that didn't make much sense for a while. But I didn't know how to reach you. And to be honest, I wasn't sure if you didn't know... or didn't care."

Didn't care. The words lodged in my throat.

She continued, "She did speak to my son a couple of years ago. I'm not sure what they discussed, but let me give you his number. Please keep me posted. Your mom's a lovely woman."

I thanked her, hung up, and sat there.

She wasn't wrong.

I did not know what was going on.

And I hadn't asked.

That part stung more than I expected.

And honestly, before now, I had kept my distance. I had let the space between us widen because it was easier. Cleaner. Less complicated.

But this was the moment. No more looking away. No more excuses. It was time to show up.

I called her son.

He remembered my mom immediately. "Yes," he said. "We took care of her Power of Attorney and healthcare directives. You're the named agent. I'll send everything over to you today."

I had the paperwork. I had the authority.

And now—I could do something.

I toured assisted living facilities across Chicago, tasted meals, asked directors questions, trying to see the place through her eyes.

Would she feel safe here?

Would she hate this wallpaper?

Would she recognize any part of this as home?

I selected a facility and her new room. Moved furniture. Hung her favorite art. Set out photos, keepsakes, and her favorite mug. I was trying, urgently, to create a space that felt familiar. Somewhere soft to land when the world around her started to disappear.

In between visits to assisted living centers, I checked in with the psych ward.

"She's doing fine," the nurse told me. "Making friends.

Taking tests. The doctor will contact you when the results are in."

"When?"

"Soon. Do what you need to do. She'll be fine. You'll see her soon."

On Saturday night at 10:00pm, the phone rang. It was the doctor.

"Hello. We're ready for you to see your mom, and I'll give you the diagnosis. Be here first thing in the morning, by seven."

"Is she okay?"

"We'll talk in the morning."

"Is she alive?"

"Yes. See you then."

Click.

I stared at the phone. How can you leave me like this?

I didn't sleep. My brain played a loop of every worst-case scenario. When I arrived at 6:45am, the nurse buzzed me into the psych ward and pointed me toward the waiting room, a closet-sized space with two chairs, a fake plant, and artwork that must've come free with the frame.

I memorized every inch of it. It helped me breathe.

At 7:15am, the doctor entered, followed by six interns—his academic entourage. They stood in a row and stared at me. I stared back.

The doctor spoke.

"I can confirm your mother has dementia. But there's something I want to show you. In all my years...I've never seen anything like this."

He gestured for me to follow him.

We walked down the corridor in silence until we stopped in front of my mom's room.

He pressed his hand to the door.

"She's waiting for you."

I stepped in.

She was sitting on the edge of the bed, looking at the door as though she knew I was coming.

"Hi, Mom."

"Hi," she said, her voice soft.

Then I saw it.

Every inch of her skin, her gown, the sheets, the wall—covered in hand-drawn Stars of David. Blue ink. Over her face, her arms, her legs. The toilet. The floor. The mirror.

Everywhere.

She had found a pen. And she had sent out a signal.

I turned to the doctor. "Is she dying?"

"No."

"Then what is this?"

He paused. "I was hoping you could tell me."

I swallowed hard. "This is her faith. She's trying to connect. Maybe to God. Maybe to herself. Maybe just trying to say, I'm still here."

He nodded. "That's what I thought too."

He looked at me, eyes kind. "This isn't destructive. This is expressive. And she's not the only one who's ever tried to draw her way through the dark."

I looked at the interns. They all looked back at me with the same quiet sadness. No one spoke.

"She can't live alone anymore," the doctor said gently.

"I know. I found a place. She moves in tomorrow."

He nodded. "Good. For now, why don't you take her to breakfast. Spend some time together."

"Should I... should I clean her up first?"

"No. No one will notice."

He was right. This was the psych ward. They had seen much worse.

I took my mother's hand.

We walked to the dining area. Found two seats at a metal table. She introduced me—by name—to every person in the room. Some said hello. Some looked away. One woman hugged me.

We ate breakfast together.

I watched them all—their habits, their silence, their scars.

I wondered what stories had brought them here.

This was just one chapter in our story.

What were the chapters in theirs?

After breakfast, I walked Mom back to her room—her star-studded sanctuary—and told her I'd be there early tomorrow to meet her before we took her to her new apartment.

She nodded and closed her eyes.

I stood for a moment in the doorway.

The room glowed with soft light and blue ink, a galaxy of hope, memory, and faith etched across every surface.

She had sent out a signal.

And this time—I heard her.

Chapter 8
The Age Reveal

I went back to the psych ward that morning. A few patients from the dining room looked up as I walked in—slight nods, brief glances. Recognition without words. I didn't expect it.

I wasn't there for them. I was there for her. I wanted her to see me before she left—and again when she arrived. Two anchors on either end of the move.

I helped Mom get ready. She'd be transferred by ambulance.

I kissed her cheek and said, "I'll see you at the assisted living."

She nodded. No questions. No protest. A quiet kind of acceptance. Or maybe just exhaustion.

I arrived at the facility ready to meet my mom and get her settled. I walked into the director's office to let her know I was there.

She said, "You've done remarkable work. I can't remember anyone moving this fast—assisted living room rented, decorated, and ready. Congratulations on a job well done. But... we have a problem."

Her face turned solemn. Not a good sign.

"We can't admit her until we confirm her identity. The Social Security Administration has no record of your mother."

I blinked.

"What?"

"We need to verify her information before we can complete the admission."

I had seen her Social Security checks for years. She absolutely had an identity. "She's been getting Social Security checks forever. That must be a mistake."

The director handed me the phone. "That's what we think. We've already dialed the office. They're expecting you."

The woman on the line said, "Hello, thank you for reaching out. We have to verify a few details."

Fine. I could manage that.

Name? Check.

Address? Check.

Birth month and day. Easy.

Then came the year.

I gave it to her.

Pause.

"I'm sorry—can you repeat that?"

I gave it again.

Another pause. Longer this time.

"And just to confirm…what year did you say?"

Okay, now I was suspicious.

I repeated it for the third time, each word slower than the last.

She replied, "We have a slightly different year."

"No," I said, my voice firm. "That's impossible. I'm giving you the year that's on her driver's license. That's the year I've known my entire life. I wasn't with her when she filed for Social Security, but I—"

And then I paused.

A weird little flicker of doubt crept in.

"Wait. What year do you have?"

She told me.

My mother wasn't 85.

She was 90.

She erased five years in five seconds.

I froze, staring at nothing, while my brain rearranged every birthday, every milestone, every medical form I'd ever filled out for her. She had shaved five years off her age—and kept the story going for decades.

"Well," the woman said, "she gave us the right number."

Of course she did.

And just like that, the system recognized her.

She existed. Officially.

Mom arrived at the assisted living facility by ambulance. I met her at the door.

The director greeted us and began the official tour. Mom's face was tight, her expression guarded. She scanned the halls, uncertain and still.

I walked her to the room I had tried to make feel like hers. Not perfect. Not home. But familiar enough to provide continuity.

"See, Mom? Your things are here."

She looked around quietly, then tightened her grip on my arm.

We sat on the bed.

I took a breath.

"Mom, I had the most interesting conversation with Social Security today."

She looked up, distracted. "Oh?"

"They had your name, address, birth month, and day—all correct."

I let it hang for a second.

"But the year? That was different."

She blinked.

"It appears you're 90. I thought you were 85. Is that right?"

For a second, she looked caught. Her eyes widened just slightly.

Then she shrugged.

"So? What's a few years."

And then she giggled.

No confession. No backstory. No drama.

Just a shrug and a laugh.

I laughed too. Of course, she lied. Of course, she shaved off a few years. It was so her.

Chapter 9
Can I Go Home?

I stayed in Chicago for a few more days. There were things to settle—questions no one else could answer. I took her legal papers to the bank and began piecing together the fragments of a life she had kept mostly to herself. I visited Mom every day while in Chicago.

On our last visit, I told her I'd be back soon.
"Will you be back tomorrow?"
"No, but I'll be back in the next few weeks."
"Can I go home?"
"No, Mom. This is your new home."
She stopped and looked at me with sad eyes. Held her close.
"I love you, Mom. I'm here for you."

That night I flew home. The next morning: back to the office, the emails, the never ending to do list. Only now, my day was sprinkled with new interruptions:

"Your mom needs toothpaste. Can you get it?"

I called my cousin: "Can you help me? She needs toothpaste."

The next day—

"She needs underwear."

Call cousin.

This continued:
She needs X? Call cousin.
She needs Y? Call cousin. Again.
On and on and on.

When the assisted living director called again, I said, "Can you make a list of everything she needs? I'll be in Chicago in two weeks and will take care of it all then." "That will be great. Thank you."

When I told my boss I'd be gone for one week to pack up her apartment, he said, "Good. We need you here."

Made the drive to Chicago. First stop: Mom.
Visited when I could, squeezed between packing and deadlines.
During those visits, she asked the same questions.

"Can I go home?"
"Mom, this is your new home."
"Can I go to my apartment? I want to go home."
"No, Mom. You're not well. You can't live on your own. This is your home now."
"Can I live with you?"
"No, Mom. I don't live in Chicago. You'd be alone all day, and that's not safe. I want you to live in a place that's beautiful, where people can take care of you every day."

I spoke to her like she was still fully capable of understanding. Over time, I realized...she wasn't. Even so, I kept explaining, hoping repetition could undo reality.

I had built a plan: calls, visits, lists. But none of it was enough.

Life wasn't pausing.

One week later, I packed up her apartment, donated what I could, cleaned, and released the space that held her last semblance of independence.

There was one thing I couldn't leave behind.

An oil painting—bought by my parents in San Francisco before I was born. A cliff overlooking the ocean, the sky-streaked gray like a storm was always coming. It hung in our living room in the only home I knew growing up. It hung on the wall of her apartment in Chicago. I wrapped it carefully and took it with me.

On my last visit before heading back to Dallas, I brought her flowers.
"I'll see you soon," I said.

In my mind, "soon" meant six months.
But reality had other plans.
The following week, I was back at work when the director of the assisted living facility called.

"Your mom ran away."

She had walked right out the front door. The aides ran after her.
She was trying to walk home—twenty miles away.
"Will you talk to her?"
Of course.

They handed her the phone.

"Hello, Mom."
A small voice: "Hello."
In the background, I heard the director coaxing: "Your daughter is on the phone. Just talk to her."

I told Mom she needed to stay in the facility—it was safe, she couldn't walk out on her own.
She asked again, "Can I go home?"
"No, Mom. Your apartment is empty. This is your new home."
Silence.
"Okay."

The next day, same call.
"Your mom walked out the front door again. She wants to go home."
I tried to reason with her over the phone, but it never stuck.
"I want to go home."
"Can I come live with you?"
My answer was always the same: "No."

I didn't want my mom near me. I had moved away to escape her judgment—and to live my life.

I pictured what her presence would require—from my life, from my freedom.

The right thing, the easy thing, was to keep her in Chicago. Visit once or twice a year. And that was that. But the calls didn't stop. Every day, the same conversation:

"Mom, no. You can't live with me. That's not a good idea. I can't take care of you."
And then, after weeks of this, I knew.
She needed more attention than I could give her from a thousand miles away.
She was my responsibility—a labor of love I didn't ask for but couldn't ignore.

I started looking at assisted living facilities in Dallas. Found one close to my office—they had space, and they could take her. That was all I needed to know.

The next time Mom asked, "Can I live with you?"
I said, "Yes. I'm bringing you to Texas to be close to me. I'll get to see you every day."
"I am happy."

Seven weeks after I first moved her into assisted living in Chicago, we were on the move again—this time, to Dallas.

The day we left, we walked out of the facility hand in hand. In the taxi, through the airport, past security—I felt like one of those parents with a bungee cord strapped to their kid's wrist.
Except this time, I was the parent—and she was the one tethered to me.
We boarded the plane together, headed for her new home.

Chapter 10
Your Mom Is a Thief

We landed in Dallas and walked off the plane, still hand in hand.

Through the terminal, into baggage claim, out to the curb—still tethered like parent and child. My best friend pulled up, jumped out of her car, and wrapped me in a hug before helping us into the backseat.

We drove directly to the new assisted living facility. Mom's room was lovely. The oil painting from Chicago —the cliff, the ocean, the storm-gray sky—hung above her bed again. I hoped it would give her a sense of familiarity.

I assumed once I dropped her off, gave her a snack, and changed her clothes, I could slip back into my normal life. But normal had been indefinitely postponed.

Mom drifted the halls—adrift, unsure of her own path.

I was working. She was alone. She started following the housekeeper up and down the halls, the only person she saw regularly.

Four weeks after I moved her in—early October, the director of the assisted living facility called.

"You need to come in. Now."

I asked if Mom was okay.

The director replied, "Yes."

I went as soon as I could.

I arrived later that day and walked into the office. The director stood as I walked in, sizing me up like a school principal about to expel a failing student. My stomach dropped. I knew something was wrong.

"Your mother is a thief," she said. "She went into another resident's room and took a sweater. We cannot have that type of behavior here. You'll need to move her out immediately."

Excuse me?

I stood there, mouth agape, feeling the heat rise into my throat.

I may be small, but I'm fierce.

No one calls my mother a thief and throws us out of anywhere. I wasn't about to let some uptight administrator tarnish our name—my name—without a fight.

I stood my ground.

"She has dementia. She probably didn't know where she was or whose sweater it was. Maybe she was cold. Maybe she thought, 'problem/solution.' She's not a thief."

It didn't matter. The director—part warden, part headmaster—was unmoved.

"This is a violation," the director said. "We need to figure out what to do."
She suggested I hire someone to monitor my mom full time.

I said no.
"I'll talk to her and set boundaries. She'll listen—we're family. I'm sure it won't happen again."

And somewhere in that fight, something shifted. For the first time, I referred to her as "family." That caught me off guard.

Wasn't this the same woman I'd left Chicago to escape? The same one I swore I'd never live with.

Yes. But now, I was defending her.

We were a unit. Somehow, we'd become a "we."

The director gave me four more weeks.

I took the win and walked out with a smile I didn't feel.

By early November, I was back in that office.

Mom had walked out the front door of the facility.

I asked how they could allow this to happen. The director glared; her verdict was harsher this time.

"She needs memory care," she said flatly. "A secure unit. Locked down. Staff trained for this. She can't stay here."

Her tone wasn't cruel. Just... final.

I shared my story—three moves in six months, an only child trying to hold it together. I just needed a few more weeks. Time to find a new place, hire movers, do it right.

She agreed to let Mom stay until late December, but I had to hire someone to sit with her daily and make sure she didn't leave—or "borrow" anything else.

Yes, thank you. I walked out exhausted and defeated.

I was the responsible party—no safety net, no backup. Just me.

During the day I worked. At night, I toured memory care facilities. Clipboards, questions, notes. One after another.

Eventually, I found one close to home. It was bright, safe, and filled with activity. 50s music played on the speakers, aides greeted residents by name, old movies flickered on the TV. The doors were locked—no way in or out without a code.

She'd be safe. She'd be seen.

This was our third try. I needed it to work.

I moved in her belongings before she arrived. The painting now hung above a couch in her room.

This facility was different. And I hoped it would be enough.

Chapter 11
Dementia Is....

She was settling into memory care. Now, I had to settle into my role.

Dementia is my new job title.

Caregiver.
No training. No handbook. Just the silent promotion that comes when watching someone you love need more than you ever expected to give. There's no clock-in, no paycheck, no team to lean on.
Only decisions. Coordination. Appointments.
And questions that keep you up at night.
What does she need?
What am I missing?
Am I doing this right?

Every day brought a new task, a new responsibility, a new version of "figure it out."
And while the rest of my life kept moving—work, deadlines, bills—I was also learning to manage someone else's life from the inside out.
It wasn't just caregiving. It was another full-time job, with no off switch.

Dementia is an unraveling.

It started small.
She'd forget what day it was. Ask the same question twice.
Month to month, then week to week, little details began to slip.
Not big things—not yet.
Just enough to notice.
Just enough to feel the shift.
I wasn't watching her disappear.
I was watching her change.

Dementia is funny.

Not all the time. Not often.
But sometimes—out of nowhere—something would happen that made me laugh so hard I couldn't breathe.
Early on, my mom started eating everything in sight. Good food, junk food, and all of it. She put on weight —enough that it was noticeable.
It reminded me of the freshman fifteen.
One day, I was helping her shower. She looked at herself in the mirror, then turned to me, dead serious, and said,
"Do you think I'm pregnant?"
I bit my lip, held my breath, and answered as calmly as I could:
"No, Mom. I don't think so."
Then I walked out into the hallway and howled.
It was one of those moments.
Completely absurd. Completely human.
Dementia is like that sometimes.

Dementia is history.

In memory care, time is fluid.
Some residents cradled baby dolls like newborns.
Others rocked gently to old jukebox songs or
whispered to people who weren't there.
I watched one woman stroke the sleeve of a military
jacket for twenty minutes, lost in a memory none of us
could see.
These weren't random behaviors.
They were anchors—touchpoints from a time they
remembered best.

Dementia is small wins.

Around the holidays, the staff set up a cookie-
decorating table in the common room.
Most of the residents just stared at the blank cookies
in front of them, unsure what to do.
My mom included.
I was the only outsider in a room full of staff and
residents.
So I got up. Went around the room. Poured sprinkles
into open hands, guided fingers, laughed, decorated.
Cookie by cookie, smile by smile.
Then we ate our art.
That day, I didn't fix anything. I didn't solve dementia.
But I created joy.
In that moment, it was enough.

Dementia is scary.

I didn't know what was coming.
I didn't know what to expect.
I didn't have answers—I didn't even know what questions to ask.

Chapter 12
Finding Light in the Fog

Dallas had been hectic, a diagnosis, a move, and a new normal.

She had care. I had questions.

Two years later, I still hadn't stopped thinking: Now what?

For two years, I buried myself in research—desperate to fix her.

There had to be something, some treatment, some strategy, some miracle that could bring her back.

Pages of notes filled my desk, research, forums, articles, chat groups, and medical papers that I barely understood, searching for something, anything that would help her. But the more I read, the more the truth sank in:

There was no cure.
No outsmarting dementia.
I am not a doctor. I am not a scientist.
I am her kid.

And if I couldn't fix this, then I had to figure out how to show up for her—and for me—in the best way possible.

I attended seminars led by professionals who spoke about the disease with certainty. They explained that dementia was progressive, that over time, my mom would become less of who she was. No treatment, no strategy, no amount of reasoning or love could stop its course.

At that time, she still recognized me—dressed herself, fed herself, even held conversations. Sometimes, she forgot details or drifted into moments of time travel, but for a 92-year-old, that seemed manageable. I held on to that, hoping maybe her decline would be slow—that we had more good days ahead than bad.

But the seminars painted a harsh picture of what was coming. The disease had stages, and each stage would take more of her. I left those sessions with a heavy heart, armed with knowledge but no solutions. No one could tell me how to stop it. No reasoning, no convincing, no pleading would turn back the clock on dementia.

And beyond that, the seminars never taught me how to deal with someone who had dementia. The information was factual but distant, focused on symptoms and progression rather than the everyday reality of caregiving.

I didn't need a textbook definition of the disease—I needed to know how to talk to my mom when she became confused, how to comfort her when she was scared, and how to manage the changes without losing the connection we had.

That's why I turned to others who were living this experience. Maybe the professionals didn't have the answers, but surely people who had walked this path before me did.

Maybe they had discovered a way to slow the decline or maintain their relationships despite the disease.

The memory care facility suggested a support group. Others in my position might have insights, ways to cope, strategies to manage the changes.

I attended my first session, feeling hopeful.

We sat in a circle as people shared stories of their parents —stories filled with sadness, fear, and frustration. They spoke of moments when their loved ones lashed out, forgot their names, lost control, or shut down completely. Their grief filled the room.

I waited—for answers, for hope, for someone to say, "Here's what helped me."

So, I asked, "Does it ever get better?"

A woman across from me sighed, then shook her head. "Yeah. When they die."

Those words stabbed me. Was that all I was supposed to hope for?

My stomach dropped. Was that it? The only relief came when it was all over?

They weren't just mourning the past; they were trapped in grief for the future.

Something in their voices unsettled me.

They talked as if their loved ones were already gone. As if they were burdens instead of people still deserving love, dignity, and connection.

I couldn't do that.
I wouldn't do that.

I just didn't want to grieve what was being lost. I wanted to fight for what was still there.

I knew this journey would be hard. I knew there would be moments of exhaustion and heartbreak. But as I sat there listening, the words running through my mind were clear: This is not going to be my reality.

I refused to believe that the rest of my mom's life would be defined by grief.

Yes, the situation was heartbreaking. Yes, I wished it weren't happening.

But it was happening. And I had to figure out how to face it—without losing her or myself in the process.

If this was our reality, if this was what the rest of our time together was going to look like, then I was going to make the best of it... somehow.

I left the meeting believing that if I tried hard enough, I could find a way.

Solving problems was second nature. There had to be a way to reach my mom, to connect with her, to make this experience something other than a slow, painful goodbye.

But dementia wasn't something to fix. It was something to face.

And I wasn't ready to accept that yet.

I was not done searching.

Because I had to find a way.

There's no magic fix.
But there is a choice in how you face it.
And that choice? That's everything.

I wasn't done searching—for her, for us, for something real beyond grief.
And I knew it was time to try again.

Chapter 13
Becoming Calm and Confident... Or So I Thought

I tried research. I tried group conversations with other children of parents with dementia.
Neither gave me what I needed: how to deal with my mom as she changed.

So, I took a different approach. Maybe if I reasoned with her—proof, evidence, facts—she'd snap back. A moment of clarity, a return to normal, whatever normal was at this point in her life.

When she talked about being in Chicago, I proudly presented the local newspaper as undeniable proof that she was, in fact, in Dallas, Texas. That should do it, right?

Nope.
She would pause, glance at the paper, then go right back to talking about her life in Chicago.

Heavy sigh.
Fine. Let's try a different angle.

When she said it was 1980 instead of 2010, I pointed to the calendar—anything to pull her into now. She'd stop, look at me with what I hoped was realization, and then... continue as if my rock-solid proof meant nothing.

Another heavy sigh.

Logic didn't land. Not once.
She wasn't going to get it.
What now?

I started watching the caregivers and the director at her assisted living facility.
They made it look easy.
They weren't arguing, they weren't proving anyone wrong, and they certainly weren't sighing their way through conversations. They were just... going with the flow.
And somehow, it worked.

Sometimes, it was brutal. I'd get frustrated, step out of the room, take a deep breath, and remind myself that this was not a battle I could win with facts. I needed to figure out how they did it.

So, I asked.

Turns out, the directors were certified assisted living managers. Certified. That had to be the secret. They were qualified; I was not.

So, I signed up—figuring if I learned what they knew, maybe I could manage things with Mom with more calm. More confidence.

Twenty-four hours of online training, passed the test, and just like that I became certified. But was I qualified?

Chapter 14
Repeat, Repeat, Repeat—STOP

Mom's story was frequently stuck in a loop.

Like the needle in a vinyl record, she kept repeating the same verse. Over. And over. And over.

The only variation?

The story of the day and my mood.

During one visit, we were sitting in the social room when she got caught in her "story loop."

She didn't pause.
Didn't take a breath.
Didn't miss a beat.

By the fifth time through, my patience wore thin. "I heard you the first time."

She paused.
Stared.
Took a breath...
And then picked up exactly where she left off.

I blinked.
Wait—what?
She hadn't even registered my frustration.

By the sixth time, I snapped.

"I HEARD YOU!"

My voice was loud.
Too loud.

I turned, expecting stares.

Instead, nothing. No one even looked up.

The aides were used to this.
I, on the other hand, was not.

I ran out the front door of the facility, into the rain.
The weight of what had just happened crashed down harder than the storm outside.

I slid into the car and just sat there, hands gripping the wheel, watching the drops hit the windshield in endless streams.

Mortified.
Ashamed.
Not at Mom.
At myself.

I tried everything.
Support groups. Research. Training. Certification.
I studied like my life depended on it—then failed when hers did.

And here I was—screaming at my mother in public.
Failing the only test that actually mattered.

What was wrong with me?

I don't know how long I sat there, frozen but buzzing
under the surface.
The rain blurred everything outside, but the real storm
was inside my own head.

Finally, I put the car in gear and drove home.
Automatic.
Numb.
Not because I didn't feel—but because I felt everything
all at once and couldn't hold it.

Pulled into the garage.
Shut the door behind me.

Walked straight upstairs, into the closet.
I didn't even turn on the light.
I moved to the farthest corner, curled up small, trying
to disappear.

Not hiding from the world.
I was hiding from myself.

The tears came—not violently, not screaming—just
steady.
I wasn't broken. I wasn't lost. I was just... empty.

I cried until there was nothing left to cry about.
And then, without even realizing it, I fell asleep.

And somewhere in that quiet, I heard it:
Be quiet. Watch. Listen. Travel.
Be quiet. Watch. Listen. Travel.

Over and over.
Until it stopped.

When I woke up, something had shifted.
I felt clean, like space had been cleared.
I remembered hearing those words—*be quiet, watch, listen, and travel*—though I didn't know what they meant.

Not yet.
But they felt like direction.

Chapter 15
Is This the End?

After that night in the closet, I gave up trying to fix everything.

I didn't have a plan.
I didn't have a strategy.
I just kept showing up.

For the next year, I visited Mom at the assisted living facility.
Sometimes I had hope.
Sometimes I just showed up.

Waiting for anything.
Hoping for more.
But mostly, I learned how to sit with what was.

The grand transformation I secretly hoped for never came.
So, I decided to try something radical: being calm.

I figured if I just sat with her—patient enough, quiet enough—maybe I'd crack the code on this new version of us.

Most visits followed the same pattern.

I'd sit with her, we'd hold hands, and I'd talk—a lot.
I talked. She listened.

That was the deal.
Updates about my life, my job, my friends, my dogs—
anything to keep the rhythm going.

She didn't respond much, just listened with a soft smile
and a gentle squeeze of my hand, happy simply because
I was there.

I told myself that was enough.

Then one day, I walked into the memory care facility
and the director asked to see me.

You never want to hear that.

She led me into her office and got right to the point.

"Your mom is losing weight."

I felt my stomach drop.

"She's in good health," she reassured me, "but she's lost
about ten percent of her body weight, which qualifies
her for hospice care."

Hospice.

The word hit hard. No warning.

Hospice meant end-of-life care.
It meant this was happening faster than I thought.
It meant....

She must have seen the panic on my face because she held up her hand.

"I know it sounds frightening, but your mom's okay. She's just slowed down her intake. She's still eating, just not like before."

My breath steadied slightly.

"The reason I'm bringing up hospice care isn't because she's dying," she said. "It's because it will actually help you. Hospice covers necessities—bed pads, personal care items, more one-on-one attention. A hospice nurse will check on her weekly. It's a good thing."

I sighed before I could stop it.
If this meant better care for her, then fine.

"Tell me what I need to do," I said, still trying to process.

A few forms, a signature, and just like that—my mother was in hospice care.

Before I left, the director added, "Eventually, she may need to move to a smaller memory care facility, but not yet. I'll let you know when that time comes."

"How long?" I asked.

"Maybe six months."

A new clock started ticking.

I nodded and left the office to find Mom.

I thought hospice would be the biggest shift.

I was wrong.

Chapter 16
My World Is Getting Smaller

I walked out of the director's office still reeling, trying to process what hospice really meant.

I took a breath, turned the corner, and found Mom sitting quietly in her room, waiting.

She sat on the edge of her bed, gazing out the window—so still, she looked like she had drifted somewhere else entirely.

For a moment, I just stood there. Watching her. The sunlight traced the soft lines of her face. She had always been strong, active, walking five to seven miles a day, attending the symphony alone, navigating the city like she owned it. Now she sat quietly, waiting.

I sat down beside her on the bed and gently took her hand in mine.
Her fingers, warm and wrinkled, curled around mine with a softness I hadn't felt in a long time.

She turned and met my gaze. Her eyes were clear.
"Hello, Glenna," she said softly, fully aware of me, of herself, of this moment.
I hadn't seen her this lucid in weeks. Maybe longer.

And then, in a voice so quiet it barely broke the silence of the room, she said something I'll never forget: "I can feel my world getting smaller. The box is closing in. What's happening to me?"

The air left my lungs.
The question I had dreaded.

I met her eyes, steadying myself, searching for the right words, the honest ones, the compassionate ones.

I had never told her about her disease. Not directly. Not like this.

But now I had to.

I squeezed her hand.
"Mom, you're right. It must feel like that," I said gently. "You have dementia. It affects how the brain works. It makes your world feel smaller because it affects memory and thinking over time."

She blinked slowly, taking it in.

I kept going, carefully.

"There are different stages—early, middle, and late-stage dementia.
Right now, you're in the middle stage. Some days, like today, you're fully here with me. Other days, you're somewhere else—another time, another place.
But wherever your mind takes you, you're always happy, healthy, and at peace."

Her fingers tightened around mine.

So, I whispered, "It might feel like your world is getting smaller.
But you're not lost. You're still you."

She nodded slowly, her lips pressing together.

And then she asked the hardest question I'd ever had to answer.
"Is there a cure? Can I get better?"

My chest tightened.
I felt the words rise, but I didn't want to say them.
I wanted to protect her.
But this was one of those rare, unfiltered moments of clarity.
She deserved the truth.

I took a deep breath.
"Mom...no. There's no cure. Not yet. Maybe one day.
But not today."

She didn't flinch. She just listened.

"There are medications that can sometimes slow the progression, but they're not an option for you at your age and at this stage. I'm so sorry."

Quiet filled the room—heavy, but not cold.
I waited, unsure of how she would process it.

Then, her voice broke the silence.
"I'm scared. I don't know what the future holds. What will I become? Who will I become?"

Her voice cracked something open in me.

I swallowed hard, blinking back tears.
"Mom... I'm scared too. I don't know what the future holds either."

I felt the tears building, but I stayed with her, leaning closer.

"But I do know this: you'll always be you. No disease can take that away.
And I'm going to be right here—side by side.
I brought you to Dallas so we could face this together.
You can't get rid of me, Mom. We're stuck together like glue. Always holding hands."

The tears came quietly.
Hers. Mine.

She leaned her head gently against my shoulder, and we just sat there—

Holding hands.
Facing the same truth.
Feeling the weight of a future, we couldn't stop.

I didn't know what would come next.
Neither did she.

But for once, we weren't lost.
We were just here.
Side by side.
No illusions.
No pretending. Just two people holding on to what was still real.

Chapter 17
A Day at the Beach

That day started like so many others—but then it wasn't.

I visited my mom at the memory care facility, our time together marked by routine. I'd help her with lunch or dinner, share updates from my life, and hold her hand in long stretches of silence. Conversations had become lopsided—me talking, her listening, the words bouncing off her like echoes in an empty room.

Now and then, she'd respond—sometimes with a clear, sharp comment. But more often, her thoughts drifted. She'd speak in bits and pieces, snippets of stories or questions that didn't quite land, like she was halfway between two places. I began to wonder if these visits were more for me than for her, as if my presence mattered only to ease my own guilt.

That afternoon, after lunch, I wheeled her into the TV room, a place as uninspired as it sounds. Dim, yellow light pressed against dark wood paneling. Linoleum floors scuffed from too many wheelchairs. Overstuffed chairs slouched in front of a big-screen TV playing an old John Wayne movie on low volume, the kind of background noise that filled the space but was never heard.

A few residents sat scattered throughout the room, some dozing, others staring blankly. The only sound was the quiet hum of the television mixed with the rhythmic click of the wall clock.

I parked her wheelchair next to me, already expecting the usual: more silence.

Then, something happened.

She leaned back in her wheelchair and tilted her face toward the fluorescent lights above. Her shoulders lifted with a deep, deliberate breath, then slowly fell with a long, audible sigh.

And then, the faintest smile.

"I love the sun," she whispered.

I blinked, startled. Her voice was so soft but so... clear.

Her eyes stayed closed, her face calm.

"I love the sand on my toes. The smell of the water. Even when it's cold, it's peaceful."

I felt my chest tighten, a sudden wave of panic rising in my throat. Was this the end?

I had read about how, sometimes, people experience vivid memories just before they die. The tunnel, the life review. This sounded so much like that.

I scanned her face, watching for the smallest change in her breathing, listening for anything out of place. But she wasn't fading. She wasn't struggling.

She was alive.

More present than I had seen her in years.

I leaned closer, my heart pounding. "Are you...at the beach?"

Her expression shifted, not in surprise, but as if I had asked the most obvious question in the world.

"Yes."

I hesitated. "Are you alone?"

She smiled, so serene. "No. I'm with Amy."

Amy. Her best friend. Her sorority sister. A name I hadn't heard in years.

I was afraid to break the spell but pressed on. "Which beach?"

"Chicago," she said without hesitation.

I stared at her, this 90 something year old woman slouched in a wheelchair under artificial light, yet completely transported. Not just recalling a memory—she was living it.

I felt the question catch in my throat. But I had to ask.

"How old are you?"

Her face softened, eyes still closed, as if she were revealing a secret meant only for herself.
"I'm 22."

My mouth hung open. And just like that, time folded in on itself.

She wasn't an elderly woman in a memory care facility. She was young. Carefree. Sitting on a beach with her best friend, toes in the sand, the world stretched wide before her.

"Is this your first time at the beach with Amy?" I asked, careful not to disrupt whatever magic was unfolding.

She let out a soft, girlish laugh. A laugh.

"Oh no," she said, almost playfully. "We've been lots of times. We have fun."

Fun.

That word landed harder than I expected.

My mom didn't talk about fun. Not the way I knew her. Life, for her, had always seemed like a series of responsibilities—serious, heavy, important work. Fun was an afterthought. And yet here she was, so light. So radiant.

I swallowed the lump rising in my throat. "What do you do at the beach?"

Her smile grew, her voice dipping into that younger version of herself I'd never met.

"We talk. We eat the food we packed. We look at the water and the waves." Then, with another quiet giggle, she added, "And sometimes... we look at boys."

And then—she posed.

Knees tilted, shoulder dropped back, chin lifted just slightly. Subtle, but unmistakable. My mother, flirting.

I almost laughed aloud, but it caught, sticking somewhere behind my ribs.

"Are you dating any of these boys?" I teased, desperate to keep the moment alive.

Her eyes were still closed. She shook her head, almost embarrassed. "Oh no. I'm too shy."

Shy.

Shy?

That word felt so foreign coming from her lips. My mom, shy? The same woman my friends had once turned to for guidance, the one they trusted with their secrets and sought out for her calm, level-headed wisdom?

But at that moment, she wasn't the composed matriarch I had always known.

She wasn't the mother who had raised me, the caregiver, the problem-solver.

She was 22, sitting on a beach with her best friend, afraid to talk to boys.

Vulnerable.
Playful.
So beautifully young.

I sat there, heart thundering, completely still.

In that moment, I stopped trying to anchor her to the present. For years, I had fought her drifting mind, trying to fix something I didn't fully understand. But this was different.

The time travel that had once frustrated me brought her peace.

I had just become a witness to a memory that brought joy to a woman whose disease I could not cure.

My mom loved the water. Always had. She would walk for hours along the shore, letting the waves soothe her spirit.

But this moment was more profound.

She wasn't walking or listening to waves. She was in a wheelchair, bathed in fluorescent light.

And yet, I had traveled with her—back to the sand, the sun, and the sound of the water in her soul.

Chapter 18
Back to the Beach

I had to return to the beach.

After that extraordinary day at the beach when Mom was suddenly 22 again, flirting, giggling, reliving a moment of joy with her best friend, I became determined to find my way back there with her.

That memory had lit her up from the inside, as if she had stepped straight into the past and pulled the sunshine with her.

I wanted more of that. I wanted her back.

So, I tried. I tried everything I could think of.

On my next visit, I opened with, "Are you at the beach today?"

She blinked, her brow furrowing.

"No," she said flatly, her eyes scanning the room as if I'd just asked if we were on Mars.

Okay, new approach.

"Mom, are you 22 again?"

Her eyes narrowed, darting back and forth—like a tiny computer searching for the right file. Then her gaze fixed, her expression stilled, and the spark faded.

She sighed softly, a quiet signal that the moment was gone. The conversation was over.

She wasn't upset. She wasn't distressed. But she couldn't make sense of my question.

I had confused her.

The hardest part? I left that visit feeling like I had failed her.

That beautiful, vivid memory of the beach, it felt like a gift when it happened, but now it was locked away again, as if the tide had washed it back out to sea.

I wanted to rewind time, to drop us back onto the warm sand together, but that wasn't how her mind worked.

I wasn't in control of the destination. She was.

That's when I realized—I was chasing one moment, instead of learning how to follow where her memories led.

If I wanted to reach her, I needed to stop directing the time travel and start paying attention to the signs she was already giving me.

So, I stopped asking and started observing.

Some days, she sat up straighter. Her voice had a lighter quality, almost musical. Her skin seemed to smooth, her energy shifted, she was someone younger than the last time I saw her.

Other days, she moved slower. Her shoulders curved forward, her voice carried a different weight, she was older now.

Her posture. Her tone. Her expressions. They gave me clues about where she was in time.

I had been so fixated on taking her back to the beach that I missed the bigger picture.

She was already time traveling. I just hadn't learned how to follow.

At first, I tried guessing.

If she seemed younger, I'd say, "Are you 60 today?"

Sometimes, I got lucky. She'd smile and nod, and we'd step right into her past together.

But when I was wrong? The moment vanished. She would look at me, confused, and the connection, gone.

I learned quickly that guessing was risky. If I got it right, I was in. If I got it wrong, I lost her.

Then one day, I tried something different.

I looked at her and said, "May I ask you a question?"

She nodded. "Yes."

I took a breath. "I forgot—how old are you?"

Her eyes lit up.

She smiled.

And then she said, "Guess."

Let the game begin.

Chapter 19
The Accidental Game

Guess.

I wasn't prepared for that.

I had asked a simple question, "May I ask you something —how old are you?" and instead of answering, she turned it into a game.

I didn't know the rules. I didn't know the stakes. I didn't even know if I wanted to play.

But there I was, winging it.

"Okay... Are you 80?"

"No!"

She looked offended.

"Oh, are you 75?"

"No."

"Younger?"

"Yes."

We went back and forth.

"Are you 74?"

"No."

"73?"

"No."

"72?"

She nodded.

And just like that, she became 72. Not just in number, but in presence. Her posture straightened. Her face softened. She looked different—not physically, but in energy. It was as if she had stepped fully into that version of herself.

I leaned in. "Where are you?"

"At home," she said, without hesitation.

"Where is your home?"

She thought for a moment. "Skokie."

Just like that she was in the house I grew up in. "Your house looks beautiful. Can you give me a tour?"

"Of course. This is the living room."

"Can you describe it? What does the living room look like?"

She smiled. "Oh, we have a dining room table with a large statue, a green couch, a piano against the wall, and lamps with crystals."

I almost laughed remembering those ugly crystal lamps.

She walked me through the entire house, the den with the flowered leather couch and the little wooden bench. We walked past my bedroom, the black fur bedspreads on my twin beds and the yellow metal bookcase holding my record player and stacks of albums. Every detail, perfect.

"Is there a basement?" I asked, testing her.

"Of course! Let's go downstairs." She described it all—the bar, the tile floor, the couches, the Christmas lights strung along the ceiling.

She was there. Fully. Completely. It was as though she had taken pictures and handed them to me through colorful descriptions.

This was it. This was how I could reach her.

She was time traveling. And now, I had found the way to go with her.

That one simple question—How old are you?—was the key.

I would start each visit by asking that question. Wherever she landed, that's where we would go.

But first, I had to learn how to play the game.

Chapter 20
The Art of the Game

When we learn a game—football, mahjong, bowling—
the first thing we learn are the mechanics.
How to keep score, how to shuffle, the order of play,
the penalties.
We practice until we can master the rules, and only
then—when the basics are wired into muscle memory
—do we become more sophisticated.
We add nuance.
We play with strategy, timing, wit.
We bring in the art.

This game—the one no one wants to play, the one
called dementia—is the opposite.
Here, the art comes first.
The heart leads.
The why carries you.

Because if it's your mother, your friend, someone you
love, and you're just clinging to the rules, you will get
frustrated.
You will take their responses personally.
You will say, "What the heck is the point?" and want to
give up.

That's why the art matters.
**The art frames how you need to show up to go
along for the ride.**

**It's what allows you to time travel with them
without losing yourself.
It's what builds the relationship and keeps you
from dissolving in frustration.
It's what steadies your hands when the rules
fall apart.**

Yes, there are mechanics.
Yes, there are rules you can learn—and you will, in the
next chapter.
But knowing the rules won't teach you how to stay.
It won't teach you how to be with someone when the
ground keeps shifting under both of you.

This chapter is about the part that matters more.
The art.
It is the way you play from the heart, not the head.
It's the mindset you carry, the adaptability you
practice, and the emotional presence you bring when
nothing makes sense.

It's not about winning.
It's not even about getting it right.
It's about showing up, again and again, while holding
on to what's still possible—when so much feels like it's
slipping away.

**The art of the game is about being relational—
about bringing your heart into the room with
your loved one.**

1: It's Not About You

Being a caregiver will pull you apart in ways you don't expect.
You'll feel anger you didn't know you had, grief you don't know where to put, and a version of yourself you barely recognize.
You will wish they were still the person they were.
You will wish you were still the person you were.

But here's the sharp truth:
This isn't your disease.
You are a participant.
You can walk away, breathe, and reset.
They can't.

That distinction matters.
It's what stops this from turning into your story, when it's not.
It's what keeps the focus where it belongs—on them, in the moment, however fractured or fragile that moment is.

It doesn't mean you don't matter.
It doesn't mean you don't get to feel grief, rage, exhaustion.
Judging yourself won't change what this is.

If you make it about your loss, your anger, your longing for who they were and who they are not—you will miss who they are, right now.

2: Be Flexible

Adapt to where they are, not where you want them to be. Meet them there even if "there" shifts under your feet. If you brace against their reality, or judge where they've landed, you'll break the connection before you start.

The rules will help.
They give you something to work with, to hold onto.
But they're just rules, not guarantees.

Sometimes you walk into their memory before you know their age, their year, their facts.
Be willing to time travel.
Let them pull you into the moment they're in—not the one you prepared for, not the one you hoped for.

Some days, you may have to be creative on the spot, finding a way to meet them without a map.

Expect the game to shift as the disease progresses. What you thought you knew, you'll relearn. What worked once may vanish without warning.

It's not a puzzle to solve.
It is sand that keeps shifting.

In the end, it's not about holding it all together. It's about staying open and vulnerable when it comes apart.

3: Don't Take It Personally, Hold Your Own Discomfort

Don't take it personally means when they are angry, dismissive, confused, or saying things that sting, it's not about you.
It's the disease.
It's the place their mind has landed.
It's their struggle, not a verdict on you.

You may hear things that throw you—parts of them you didn't know, didn't expect, maybe wish you didn't have to carry.
And yes, judgment shows up: Why didn't I know?
How could they?
That pull to make sense of it—to explain, to pin it down—can yank you out of the moment.

If you react—with anger, with hurt, with pulling away —you risk losing the moment of connection that's still possible.

What you hold back may matter more than what you give.

4: Be All In

There's a difference between being in the room and actually being there.
You can sit next to your mother, your partner, someone you love, and still be somewhere else— glancing at your phone, half-listening, waiting for it to be over.

They might not know the date, the details, maybe not even your name that day—but they feel when you've checked out.

Being all in takes effort.
It's not just hearing the same story again.
It's staying put when the conversation circles, when the silence drags, when nothing new is coming, and you want to pull back.
It's resisting the urge to steer or fill the gaps just to escape the weight of it.

I have left visits wiped out—not from the conversation, but from the discipline it takes to stay present.
It's not always satisfying.
It's not always meaningful.

But sometimes, just being all in is the only thing that holds the thread between you.

5: Don't Give Up

There will be days when the only word going through your mind is ENOUGH.

You've hit the wall and are moments away from losing your cool, shutting down, or running off to hide in a closet—just like I did.

This feeling comes and goes.
When your loved one becomes contentious, or doesn't know who you are, or just stares at you with no conversation, you may think...why bother?

Why do you bother?

You stay because of your bigger why.
Love, care, compassion, obligation, guilt—whatever your reason, or a mix of many, you have to keep this "why bother" front and center.

When you want to give up, remind yourself of your big why, your purpose.

It didn't feel like I had a choice.
As an only child, there was no one else.
The only choice I had was to be a caregiver or not be present.
The guilt that went with walking away would have been devastating.

I realized I had to step up out of obligation—and that turned into compassion, companionship, and true love.

When Mom passed, I was able to look back at our time together and know I did the best I could. Those nine years weren't easy, but they were filled with love, joy, and laughter.

Don't give up.

Give yourself the opportunity to look back with pride and gratitude that you were there when your loved one needed you.
You showed up despite sadness and difficulty.
You were a caregiver.
You were a warrior.
You were someone who truly made a difference—in their life, and maybe in your own.

Chapter 21
Mastering the Rules of the Game

These are the mechanics of the game.

Not the why—the how.

How to navigate moments that don't make sense. How to hold your place when theirs keeps shifting.

How to read the cues, match the pace, ask the questions that matter, and leave the rest.

Be quiet, watch, listen, travel...the words I heard in the closet were the clues that developed the art and rules of the *How Old Are You Today?* game.

The rules don't guarantee connection.
They don't promise you'll reach them every time.
But they give you something to hold onto—a
framework, a way to stay in it, a way to stay present
when the ground tilts.

These are the mechanics that helped me keep going.
Not perfectly. Not without failure.
But with just enough steadiness to keep showing up.

1-Watch the Eyes and Energy

One of the biggest breakthroughs came when I started watching her eyes.
They gave me subtle clues about where she was in that moment—what time her mind had landed on.

When her eyes moved back and forth, I knew she was searching for something in her memory. It might take a moment—or twenty. Sometimes she never landed at all.

But when her eyes stilled—when she looked straight ahead or right at me—I knew she'd landed.

That's when I understood: listening wasn't just hearing.
It was watching.
It was understanding the difference between when her eyes darted and when they fixed—between searching and arriving.

2-Protect Their Dignity

Never guess too high: a painful lesson when you get it wrong.

One day, without thinking, I blurted out, "Are you 90?"
Her face froze, and I could practically feel the heat from the glare she shot at me.
"Do I look that old?" she snapped, clearly offended.

I half-expected her to check her reflection in the mirror —just to confirm.

And just like that—conversation over. Door slammed shut. Game lost before it even began.

It took me far too long to realize that Mom's vanity wasn't gone just because her memory was.
She still saw herself a certain way, and guessing too high made her feel... old.
And nobody likes feeling old, especially my mother.

I needed to play it safe—start lower and then work my way up.
I began guessing by decades, trying to read her energy and posture before throwing out a number.

If she seemed confident, vibrant, and full of life, I might start with, "Are you 60?"
If she seemed more tired and reserved, if her chin rested closer to her chest, I'd start higher.

Once I got close, I'd zero in with five-year increments: "Are you 65? 70? 75?"
Once I hit the right range and she gave me a clue—like nodding or showing some recognition—I'd narrow it down even further.
"Older or younger?" I'd ask, then move by one-or two-year increments until we landed on the exact number.

It wasn't about identifying the number.
It was where she was anchored—in memory and body—that day.

I learned to read her energy before guessing, because it wasn't just about numbers—it was about protecting how she saw herself.

3-The Power of Touch

Once I got the game down—once I knew how to follow her into whatever time and place she was living in—I realized that sometimes words weren't enough.

Connection wasn't always about conversation.
It was about presence.

When she seemed settled, I'd reach out and gently touch her hand or her knee.
A small, simple gesture that said, I'm here.

But touch required awareness.
If she was living in a time when I was still a child, reaching out as an adult could confuse her and break the moment.

Some days, just sitting close was enough.
Other times, a light touch made her smile and linger— it anchored her.

I learned to read the moment, not force it.
Because in her world, touch wasn't just physical.
It was trust.

4-Match Their Pace

Patience didn't come naturally to me.
I had to learn how to sit through the long stretches of silence without giving in to the urge to fill the gaps.

I was wired to keep the conversation moving, to guide it somewhere, to feel like I was making a connection, and getting a result.

At first, I thought I was helping by asking follow-up questions or repeating the original one, hoping to nudge her in the right direction.
I didn't realize that my need to move things along was pulling her out of her own process.

I learned to wait—without pushing, without rushing, without feeling like I needed to get somewhere.
The challenge wasn't guiding her—it was holding back long enough to let her catch up with her process.

5-Stay Curious

Dementia scrambles how the brain handles broad or abstract ideas, open-ended questions were too much.
General questions didn't work.
If I asked, "What do you think?" or "What's going on?" she'd just look at me, her mind rifling through the file drawer of memory and coming up empty.

Direct questions gave her something to hold onto—a person, a place, a detail—and let her respond.

One time, she was in her 50s.
I asked if she had kids.
"Yes—a girl."
"What do you do with her?"
"Oh, today I'm taking her to drama class for a play rehearsal."
"What is the play?"
"Sleeping Beauty."
"What part does your daughter play?"

She gave me that familiar look—the one that said I was missing the obvious—and replied, "Sleeping Beauty."

"Describe her costume."
And she did: a long orange mohair jumper, white blouse, hair tied back with a ribbon.
Details I hadn't thought about in decades.

When I asked, "Who else is there?" she named theater friends I hadn't remembered since childhood.
She wasn't just drifting through fragments—she was fully inside that day.

6-Don't Expect Consistency

One of the most disorienting parts of the game was the inconsistency.

She might be 54 one day, waiting for Leo to come home from work.
The next time, she was in her early 30s, riding the bus to her job.
Or she was watching a soloist at the symphony.

Every visit began the same—playing the *How Old Are You Today?* game but the outcome was never the same.

It took practice to walk in without expectations—to just let her land where she was that day.

Once I did, I realized adapting to her reality was the only way to make the most of our time together.

She reset every time, and I had to be present, patient, and willing to time travel with her, wherever she went.

Chapter 22
54 and No More

I thought I had it down.
I was wrong—but not defeated. Just...reminded.

When I discovered that asking Mom's age could open a door to conversation, I thought I had finally figured something out.
It felt like real progress, like I'd cracked part of the code.

But the next visit reminded me just how unpredictable this journey could be.

I sat beside Mom, just as I had before, and opened with the same question that had worked each time I visited.

"I'm sorry—I forgot. How old are you?"

She blinked, tilted her head slightly. Then her eyes brightened.

"Guess!" she said, with that playful spark I was starting to recognize.

By now, I knew better than to just pick a number at random. I studied her energy, her face, her eyes. Today her eyes were bright, and she sat taller, so I guessed a younger age.

"Are you 65?"

She shook her head.

"Older or younger?"

"Younger."

"60?"

"Younger."

"55? No."

"Younger?"

"Yes."

She smiled, confident: "I'm 54."

And just like that, she was 54. Not just in age, but in the way she held herself and how she spoke. Her voice carried confidence that I hadn't heard in a long time.

I leaned in, curious.

"Where do you live?"

Without missing a beat, she gave me the exact address of the house I grew up in, the house we sold years ago.

I nodded. "Are you married?"

She smiled. "Of course! Leo is at work."

She said it like my dad had just left for work and would be home any minute.

"Do you have any children?"

She paused, then nodded. "Yes, I have a daughter, Glenna."

I held my breath.

"Tell me about her."

"She's fourteen," she said, her voice warm. "She has long dark hair, she's on the small side, has a nice smile, and doesn't clean her room."

I smiled. That last part was true.

"Does Glenna have any hobbies?"

"Oh yes," she said, lighting up. "She sings, she takes acting and dancing classes, and she has many friends. She does a lot of shows—she was Cinderella, I was so proud!"

I smiled.

"What do you do during the day?"

She exhaled and settled back into the chair, painting a picture of her life with words.

"I always start my day reading the newspaper at the kitchen table, drinking a pot of coffee."

I could picture her instantly—sitting at that green shell table, coffee in hand. She loved that table. Mom wasn't just recalling a general habit. She was there. She did that every morning when I was growing up.

Every day, she would cut out my horoscope and slip it into my lunch bag before I left for school. I remember reaching for my lunch and pulling out a folded newspaper clipping with my daily fate printed in ink.

She didn't hesitate.

"I clean up the house a bit, then I talk to my sisters. Every day."

Of course. That was her world. A phone call with one sister, then another. By the time I got home from school, she was caught up on all the family gossip.

"What do you do when your daughter comes home from school?"

"Oh, well, I help Glenna with her homework before I start making dinner. Sometimes, her friends come over and I give them potato chips and pop."

Pop. Never soda.

This wasn't just a memory. This wasn't nostalgic. She was living it.

She wasn't reminiscing. She wasn't telling stories about "back when."

She was there.

Encouraged, I thought, this is working. Stay with her here.

Since she believed she was 54, I assumed she'd remember everything that came before that time.

So, I tried it.

"Mom, do you remember when I had my 12th birthday party in the basement? We dressed up like beatniks, and everyone wore black turtlenecks?"

It felt like the perfect choice—a vivid, personal memory we had both lived.

But she just stared at me.

Her eyes shifted, scanning my face as if trying to work out a puzzle, something didn't quite match.

I waited for recognition. A spark. Something.

Nothing.

I didn't understand it in that moment. Maybe she was tired, maybe distracted. I let it go.

I had assumed, if she believed she was 54, she could recall everything that came before that time, the life she had already lived at the age of 50 or 52.

But she wasn't moving backward through time. She was frozen in it.

Her memory didn't stretch back to gather all the previous years or process information in the present.

That meant that at this moment, Mom thought that I was fourteen with long braids. I wasn't the grown woman sitting beside her in the memory care facility. The adult next to her wasn't the daughter she had raised.

At best, I was a visitor.
At worst, a stranger.

She saw my face.
But not me.

Chapter 23
Aiding the Aides

After I learned how to speak the language of the game with Mom, I realized it was a way in—a way to connect—for anyone walking alongside someone with dementia.

Every patient in the memory care facility has a story. Most people just don't take the time to listen.

Visitors came and went—birthdays, quick visits, guilt-driven drop-ins. But without knowing how to listen, they didn't always see the story still being lived.

The aides had jobs to do. People to care for. Schedules to keep. Listening wasn't in the job description—but it should've been.

But if you sit long enough in the dining room, if you observe, really observe—you realize: every day is a new experience.
For them. For me.

One day, a patient would slump over, dozing in their chair. The next day, they'd sit upright, feed themselves, and speak with clarity and energy. One day their skin looked like a crinkled leaf in late winter—dry, fragile, fading.

Another day, they were glowing, their faces fuller, eyes brighter. They had traveled to a younger version of themselves. And when they time-traveled, they didn't just remember youth, they became younger, in mind and body.

One woman who could barely walk stood up, gripped her walker with one hand, grabbed her purse with the other, and marched to the front door.

"I have to catch the bus," she announced.

The locked door stopped her, but not for long. She turned around, walked back to her seat, and started the process all over again.

Where was she going? What age was she that day? Who was she going to see? I'll never know. But she never made it on the bus—and it didn't matter. The anticipation, the purpose, the imagined destination... it brought her joy.

Another time, an older man scooted his chair close to a woman nearby. He reached out, stroked the back of her hand, and said softly, "I love you."

I don't know who he saw when he looked at her—a long-lost love, a wife, a dream—but in that moment, he meant it. Every word.

There was the woman with the baby doll, singing lullabies and changing diapers as the dutiful mother. She never let that baby leave her arms.

We played the *How Old Are You Today?* game, and over time, I learned that the baby liked peas and only fell asleep to one specific song. We sang it on repeat. When the trust was finally earned, I was allowed to hold the baby while she ate. And make no mistake, it was an honor.

One day, I noticed a new aide sitting at the table, overwhelmed, trying to figure out how to connect with each patient. I offered what I had learned.

"That woman loves to fold laundry," I told her. "She was a housekeeper earlier in her life. Dump a clean pile of towels on the table, she'll fold them happily, then start again. And the woman next to her spits food. Always sit to the left."

The aide blinked. "Who are you? Do you work here?"

"No," I said. "This is my mom. I like to spend time visiting with her."

The aide said, "You should teach a class or something. They seem to trust you. How do you know all this?"

I smiled, and before answering, I paused.

"For years," I told her, "visiting my mom was just another task on my to-do list. Get in, get out. She repeated the same stories, and I kept trying to correct her. It was frustrating. I thought she was broken. But one day I gave up fixing her and tried something different."

And then I told her about the game;
How it started by accident.
How it taught me to slow down.
How it made me curious instead of impatient.
How it helped me find joy when I thought I had lost it.

She listened, wide-eyed. "Will you teach me the game someday?"

"Absolutely," I said. "It's not complicated. You have to listen, watch, and care enough to try."

She smiled. "You've taught me a lot already. Thank you."

What began as a desperate attempt to connect with my mother became something more.
In helping her, I learned to help others.
And in helping others, I started to see the broader truth: we're not just visiting. We're learning.

And sometimes, we're even teaching.

Chapter 24
Better Left Unsaid

Some memories are light. Some are unexpected.
And some... should never resurface.
We all have parts of ourselves we keep tucked away.

Some memories are joyful. Some, harmless. Others we've buried so deep, we hope they never surface again.

Dementia doesn't care. It doesn't sort memories by comfort or consequence. Everything is fair game—and anything can show up at any time.

One afternoon, I walked into the memory care facility and found my mom in the hallway, yelling at a man I'd never seen before. She was two feet from him, screaming over and over, "Get away from me. Don't touch me." The man stood against the wall, clearly terrified. Four attendants were trying to intervene, physically holding my mom back.

She fought them, calling them names I'd never heard come out of her mouth. The rage was raw, and the language was violent. Eventually, they were able to guide her into the dining room, seat her at a table, and bring her a glass of water. Her body started to settle, but the room was still buzzing.

When I approached, she didn't recognize me. Her eyes were wild—disconnected, distant. Somewhere else entirely.

I didn't try to bring her back. I didn't try to anchor her. I waited.

The attendants left to set up the room for dinner, and I sat quietly across from her. Her breathing slowed. She looked younger. Still tense, but more present. Her eyes were wide open, almost reflective.

After fifteen minutes, I asked gently, "May I ask you something?"

She nodded.

"I forgot—how old are you?"

"Are you 50 years old?"

"No."

"Are you older or younger?"

"Younger."

"Are you 40?"

"No."

"Are you older or younger?"

"Younger."

"Are you 35?"

"No."

"Are you older or younger?"

"Younger."

That day, we landed somewhere around 30 or 31. She was vague—restless.

The numbers were brushing up against a time she had tried to erase.

I didn't ask any more questions. I didn't press. I knew better.

She had told me once, long ago, about a short-lived marriage. A man who tried to hurt her. A time in her life she described as "fighting for her life." We never spoke of it again.

I've always wondered—did the man in the hallway look like him? Sound like him? Was that what triggered the memory?

That day, dementia didn't bring us to a sweet spot in her history. It brought us to the one place she had fought to forget.

I realized then—she wasn't angry at the man in the hallway.

She wasn't angry at the attendants.

She wasn't angry at me.

She wasn't fighting the people in front of her—she was fighting a memory. She was wrestling with something from long ago.

Something buried for over sixty years had suddenly come roaring back.
And in that moment, her mind couldn't separate past from present.

The fear, the rage, the instinct to protect herself—it all belonged to a time long ago.

But dementia doesn't come with a timestamp.

By playing the game, I wasn't just trying to figure out her age that day—I was trying to understand what the emotion meant. Where it came from.

And once I landed on her age, once I understood where she was, the anger made sense. Some things never leave us. Even when we try to forget them.

It had a place.

And somehow, that gave me peace.

Chapter 25
You Don't Know Me

I had gotten close to her past. I'd gone there. It meant something. But it didn't prepare me for what came next.

The worst day as a caregiver may not be the day your loved one passes.
Instead, it is the day they do not know who you are.

When one person shared this in support group, the others looked on with fear in their eyes. Afraid to say it aloud but knowing their day would come.

One dreary morning, I walked into the community room at the assisted living facility. The faint smell of old age lingered in the air, not unpleasant, but unmistakable. The energy in the room was as gray as the clouds and rain outside. A muted game show played on the TV in the corner—no one watched. A few residents sat in wheelchairs, some with heads drooped forward dozing, others gazing blankly into the distance. The only people who were awake were the attendants. They stared at me. I stared at them.

And then, there was my mom.

She sat with her hands folded neatly in her lap, her chin resting softly on her chest. She looked staged—like someone had arranged her in a perfect pose of silence.

I stood for a moment, watching her. She looked peaceful —and impossibly small, as if she'd shrunk these past few days.

Then, a flinch. A small movement. A sign she would soon awaken.

I walked over and knelt beside her, placing a gentle hand on her knee.

"Hello," I said softly.

Her eyelids fluttered open, and for a second, she stared at me and did not blink. Her brown eyes—my brown eyes—held steady, but there was nothing behind them. No spark. No recognition.

It hit me like a punch to the chest. This was the moment every child dreads. The day your parent looks at you and doesn't know who you are.

I froze. My mind started spinning, grasping for something, anything, that might anchor me.

What do I do?
How do I fix this?
What if this is it?

What if she never knows me again?

The questions piled up, colliding in my head, leaving no room for calm.

And then, cutting through it all, came a voice. Loud and insistent, almost screaming in my head:

Play the game—play the game—play the game.

It wasn't just a suggestion—it was a command. My breath steadied, my hands stopped trembling, and I gripped the words like a lifeline.

"You look lovely today," I said, my voice calm but deliberate. "May I ask you a question?"

She blinked, tilting her head slightly, as if deciding whether to humor me. Then, she nodded faintly.

"I know you told me before, but I've forgotten. How old are you? Are you 70 years old?"

She squinted slightly, like the number didn't sit right in her ears.

"No."

"Are you younger?"

"Yes."

"Are you 50?"

"No."

"Younger?"

"Yes."

"Are you 30?"

"No."

"Younger?"

"Yes."

"Are you 25?"

"No."

"Older?"

"Yes."

"Are you 26?"

"Yes," she said, her voice soft but certain.

I paused. Perhaps I was imagining it, but she seemed to grow younger before my eyes. Her posture shifted, her shoulders straightened, and her chin lifted just slightly. A flicker of clarity returned to her eyes.

"Do you live with your parents?"

"Yes."

"Tell me about your room and family."

"The room is yellow. I have a twin bed and share this room with my two sisters. My brothers are in another room."

"What else is in the room?"

"There is a small closet where I keep my clothes, a chest of drawers, a lamp, and my books. I like to read."

"Are you working?" I asked gently.

"Yes," she said with pride. "I'm a teller at the bank. I count cash and help customers—I must be exact, account for every penny."

"Do you like your job at the bank?"

"Yes. It is a very important job."

"Why is this job important to you?"

"I help my parents and give them my earnings. I contribute to the house."

"That is very important. Thank you for telling me."

"How do you get to work? Do you live far away?"

"I live quite far. I take the bus every morning and afternoon. It is nice. We go along Lake Shore Drive past the museum. I always look out the window at the buildings and even catch a glimpse of the lake. It's so beautiful."

"And what do you wear to work?"

"I must look professional. A blue suit, gloves, and a matching hat," she said with a small smile, her voice growing stronger. "I wear high heels; it makes me look taller."

"You sound very professional, and I am sure you look lovely," I said, returning her smile.

She chuckled softly, and the sound filled the room with warm light.

And just like that, she started talking. She told me everything—about the customers, the accounts she balanced, and the pride she took in her work.

After a while, she became quiet, dozed off, her head nodded forward, and her chin touched her chest.

She looked just like she had when I walked in—still, chin down, folded hands.

The tightness in my chest eased, replaced with a sense of calm.

Mom did not know me because I did not exist. She had not yet given birth to me. At this time in her life, I was a stranger. A nice woman interested in her life.

But then I realized something: I still had a role to play.

If she saw me as a kind stranger, then I would be the kindest stranger she had ever met.

I would be the person who listened, who asked questions, who cared about her life—even if she had no idea, I was her daughter.

I stopped watching her fade and started following her into the life she still remembered.

So that's what I did.

And for the first time in this journey, I didn't feel like I was losing her.

I felt like I was finally getting to know her.

Chapter 26
The Final Move

The first moves were emotional.
This one was emotional—and practical.

Mom's money was running out.

I filled out piles of paperwork, worked with hospice counselors, and researched homes that would accept her with Medicaid.

Right before the holidays, I found a nursing home that had an opening.
It was bigger than her old community, more clinical, less homey.
The residents weren't just people with dementia—they were people dealing with all kinds of long-term illnesses, both physical and emotional.

At the intake meeting, the business manager said something I'll never forget.
"You know," she said, "you could have set up a trust. That way the money would've gone to you, for your future."

I paused—for about ten seconds.

And then I said, "No. This isn't my money. It's hers. It was always meant to take care of her. I'm just grateful she had it while she needed it. I have no right to it."

I was grateful.
Not resentful.
Not entitled.
Grateful.

Once the paperwork was finished, I got to work making her room feel like home.

I hung the same picture that had traveled from our house to the first assisted living facility, and then from move to move—the one that used to hang above the living room couch when I was a kid. Now it hung above her bed, a small thread tying the past to the present.

Her room looked like home.
What we did during visits made it feel like one.
The aides gave us a quiet corner—somewhere off to the side where we could still play the game, still time travel, still be together without the noise of the world crashing in.

But over time, her dementia kept progressing.
She slept more.
And slowly, swallowing became harder.

The staff recommended a mechanical diet—every meal, no matter what, pureed into uniform mush. I started calling it "space food"—trying to make it into a joke.

We laughed sometimes.
Even then.
Even there.

Every holiday, I brought her a crown to wear. Maybe the cake looked like mush—but the crown was unmistakable.

This was our fifth move—not where we thought we'd end up.

But still celebrating.
Still together.

Chapter 27
When I Met Me

The patients sat at tables in the dining room, each one covered in a scarred plaid cloth and adorned with plastic plants—a weak attempt to add beauty to a dreary environment.

Pots and pans clanged in the kitchen. Aides stacked trays of food onto silver carts. Across the room, someone shouted, "Start in the back!"

Mom was dozing; each breath brought her chin closer to her chest. An empty chair held my spot.

I sat beside her. In. Out. In. Out. I matched her breathing to pass the time.

Her eyes flickered. She stared, hands resting on her forearms, holding something unseen. That day, she looked younger and more vibrant. She had gone somewhere in her mind. I knew that place, and I knew how to meet her there.

This was my cue to play the *How Old Are You Today?* game—verbal time travel, pinpointing her timeline.

"May I ask a question?"

"Yes."

"I have forgotten how old you are. Are you 50?"

She raised an eyebrow. "Not that old!"

"Are you 40?"

"Not yet. Are you 35?"

"No."

"Are you older or younger?"

"Older."

The questions continued until we arrived at the answer.

Today, she was 39, the age when she gave birth to me.

This was sure to be an interesting visit.

"Do you have a child?"

"Yes."

"Is it a boy?"

"No."

"You have a little girl!"

"Yes."

Staring down, her arms moved closer to her chest, and she started to rock. Back and forth, back and forth.

In her mind, Mom had just given birth. The baby in her arms was me.

The clock reversed, and we traveled back in time.

It was surreal—me, a grown woman in a nursing home, simultaneously staring at my own baby form in my mother's arms.

My chest rose and fell, and my mind became clear.
Glenna, this is an amazing moment.
You are meeting you. Be present, make Mom comfortable, ask questions, and listen.

"What is the baby's name?"

"Glenna. We call her the miracle baby."

That baby was me.

My mom had several miscarriages, and my parents had given up hope of ever having a child. A baby was a dream. After all the wear and tear on my mom's body, she was going to the hospital for surgery that would ensure there would be no children. The night before the procedure, the doctor told my mom he "didn't feel right about it and wanted to run some tests."

She was pregnant.

With me.

That was why they called me the miracle baby.

"Tell me about the birth of the miracle baby."

And out of nowhere, Mom screamed, "IT HURT!"

I stifled a laugh. The dining room froze—spoons midair, aides wide-eyed.

I mouthed, "It's OK," and action resumed.

"I'm sorry it hurt," I said.

Mom replied, "It's OK. I knew what was on the other side of the pain—finally, a baby."

Tears welled in my eyes. This was the first time she had ever told me this, and it was not a past memory but a present situation.

"Do you care for the baby?"

"Oh yes, I feed the baby, wash the baby, and watch the baby sleep. I love the baby."

"Do you get much rest?"

"No. I am afraid if I go to sleep the baby will die. If I am there and awake, she will stay alive."

Her fear ensured my existence. My mind flooded with gratitude for her love and care.

I couldn't tell her I was the baby—she'd get confused. I didn't want to ruin this beautiful moment.

What came next?

I mentally begged for words that would bring her tranquility. Then the words flowed as they came from my heart and soul.

"I saw the baby. She is alive and beautiful. You are an amazing mother; you would be so proud."

Her eyes widened. The corners of her mouth rose in a smile as she put her hand on the head of her miracle baby.

We sat quietly for a moment.

I was watching her and me, as she was giving love to the imaginary baby.

Then, all energy seemed to drain from her.

She looked exhausted. The nightly vigils had taken their toll.
She had done her job—watching, protecting, keeping the baby alive. And now, she was asking for permission to rest.

"Can I go to sleep now?"

I nodded and signaled for the aides to take her to her room—to finally rest, not just for the night, but from a lifetime of worry.

Chapter 28
Buckle Up

Witnessing the past in this intense manner made the present more vivid.
It was like stepping out of a black-and-white landscape into a full color dreamscape.

The clanging of spoons and dishes became louder.
The smells of food became stronger.
The beams of sunlight became brighter.
The voices were deafening.

My eyes clenched shut, trying to lock in the memory—to hold on to every detail.

And then, the replay finished.
Time to go.

The experience shifted my balance. Every step was labored and purposeful.

I reached my car, slid into the driver's seat, and shut the door.

Mom had been afraid I would die, that she would lose me like the others that came before me. My survival was her purpose.

When I was growing up, we never discussed my birth or baby years.
I never knew.
Now, I did.

I sat frozen, staring straight ahead, but my mind was still back in that dining room, back in the past, back in the moment that had just rewritten everything I thought I knew.

Then, the flood gates opened.

A torrent of tears streamed down my face.
Like a morning shower, the tears ran down my cheeks, dripping from my chin to my chest.

I gripped the steering wheel for support, holding on as though my life depended on it.

Everything poured out of me.
The tears soaked my shirt and drained every thought from my mind.

I had nothing left.
A dry well.

I let out a long sigh and slowly became aware of my surroundings.
The car was warm.
Sunlight streamed through the windows.

The seatbelt was buckled, holding me safely inside the experience.

My cheek was rough.
My eyes felt swollen.

But the storm had passed.

I grabbed my phone and called my best friend.

I started at the beginning of the day, told her about playing the game, meeting the baby—me —and how Mom was afraid I would die, what I said in response, and the healing that followed. The words were punctuated with tears and deep breaths.

The other side of the line was quiet.

For a second, I thought she had hung up.

Then, I heard a sniffle.

And another.

Her voice cracked.
"I know how much you've struggled with your mom over the years.
I was always so concerned you would never be able to find peace.
You are so lucky to have this.
I wish I had this time with my mother.
I wish I had known about her life."

Pause, heavy breath...

"Most of us try to ask our parents about their lives, but they usually brush it off,
'That was a long time ago,' or 'It doesn't matter now.'

They don't really tell you. You just get surface."

Pause and sniffle...

"But you didn't. You lived it with her. You met your mom when she was a brand-new mother. You saw her fear, her love, her hopes—raw and unfiltered."

"Glenna, you were meant to discover this game and share it with others.
We all deserve this experience."

Chapter 29
Silent Coronation

No party. No cake. Just a crown, a spoon—and the beginning I didn't see coming.

It came quietly—on her 98th birthday. A passing of the crown.

We were alone in the private dining room.

I fed her lunch, mechanical food, pureed into anonymous shapes.

Space food.

She ate slowly, carefully. Each bite was an effort.

Spoon in one hand, her hand in the other, I stayed beside her.

Today, feeding her felt like hours. This birthday lunch was a gift.

No crowd.
No noise.
Just the two of us.

At one point, an aide stepped into the room and asked if I wanted a picture.
I said "Yes."

I reached into my bag, pulled out the plastic crown like I always did, and placed it on her head.

She looked at me—soft, clear, deliberate—and said:

"No. It's time you wore the crown."

Her words didn't come easily, but they came.

And they landed exactly where they needed to.

It wasn't just a birthday gesture. It was a quiet coronation. A moment of surrender and trust.

We played the game, shared her history, lived through this experience—and now, her time as the anchor was ending.

She was telling me—with more clarity than words ever could—that she knew what was coming.

That I would need to be steady.

That I would be the one to carry her story forward, and one day, let her go.

The crown didn't feel plastic anymore, it felt like a legacy.

It was silent preparation.

Not for her death—but for my living, without her.

The crown came off her head and settled onto mine.

The aide quietly took the picture.

In it, Mom is sitting back in her wheelchair, her arms wrapped tight around me.

My head rests against her chest, wearing the plastic crown.

It wasn't posed.
It wasn't planned.

It was her holding on.
Me holding back.

Not a birthday.
Not a tradition.

A quiet acknowledgment. A silent release.

She knew.
So did I.

It wasn't a birthday.
It was the beginning of goodbye.

Chapter 30
Five Lessons to Live By

I thought she had said all she needed to say.
I was wrong.

Each week I visited Mom for lunch. I fed her, held her hand, and talked—about everything and nothing. We had celebration rituals depending on the day or the holiday—crowns for birthdays, beads for Mardi Gras, and on Mother's Day, always a pureed cheeseburger and fries. Her favorite meal, space food style. On New Year's Day, I visited very early in the morning —I wanted to be the first person she saw to start our year together.

At 6:00am, I drove through the quiet streets toward the nursing home. The building was dim and nearly silent. The overnight aide, still bleary-eyed from the shift, woke when I entered.

"Happy New Year," I said.
"Same to you," she replied.

The halls were quiet. Patients were tucked into their beds like human burritos.
Holidays were an excuse to let them sleep in—and let the aides enjoy a moment of peace.

I walked into the room and quietly whispered hello to Mom, not wanting to startle her. She was 98, sleeping more and talking less. But that day, she was alert—her eyes open, staring at the ceiling, as if she'd been waiting.

Her energy told me she was younger than 98 today.

"I have forgotten how old you are. Are you 70?"
The corners of her mouth turned up—game on. She simultaneously shook her head and said no.
"Are you older than 70?"
"Yes."
"Are you 75 years old?"
"No."
"Older?"
"No."
"Oh, you are younger than 75?"
She smiled and said yes.

That day, Mom was 71 years old. I would have been in my early 30s.

I asked where she was that day. She told me she was sitting at the round green kitchen table inlaid with seashells, describing the flowered wallpaper and the olive-green refrigerator. She said Dad was drinking tea and eating a sleeve of pinwheel cookies while she was having another cup of coffee.

Mom painted a vivid picture of my childhood home in Skokie, Illinois—everything was as I remembered it.

"Mom, that sounds like a great way to spend New Year's Day."
She said, "Yes, just us, right here."
"Do you have any resolutions for the next year?"

"Yes. Every day I am going to make certain that I live by my five lessons."

"You live by five lessons?"

"Yes. These are the five lessons I live by. They help me live a good life."

"I have forgotten the lessons. Can you tell them to me?"

"Of course."

She spoke to each one deliberately:

- Learn something new every day.
- Laugh every day.
- Live every day.
- Say I love you every day.
- Be grateful for what you have.

"Mom, since today is New Year's Day, those will also be the resolutions I live by. Would you like to do this together?"

She looked at me, smiled, nodded, quietly closed her eyes, and fell asleep.

In fifty years of my life, that was the first time I had ever heard the five lessons I live by. I quickly grabbed a pen and wrote the lessons on the palm of my hand. They were new to me. I did not want to forget them.

At this point, she typically answered with just a word or two—she was beyond full conversations or complex thoughts.

But that day, Mom did not falter. Her voice was clear, loud, and purposeful. She was giving me a mom lesson, the kind you share with your child when they're just starting out.

I believed the words came from something bigger. Mom intended me to hear—and to live by them.

I do.

Chapter 31
Talking Without Words

There came a time when my mom could no longer speak. Her words didn't drift away. Her ability to speak them did.

She sat with closed eyes while I talked—sometimes a faint smile, a crease in her brow, or a flicker of her lids. Then she'd open those big brown eyes, and I could tell a thought was there.

Her eyes were my eyes, filled with questions, fear, and sadness.
Mom knew it too—her silences and closed eyes signaling that the end of the path was drawing near.

One day, I held her hand as she looked distant.
I asked, "Can you hear me?"
She nodded and squeezed my hand.
"Do you want company?"
She nodded and squeezed again—deliberate.
"I have an idea how we can talk."
She smiled.
"Okay. If I ask a question and the answer is yes, squeeze once. If the answer is no, squeeze twice. Got it?"
One squeeze.
Game on.

"Mom, may I ask a question?"
One squeeze.
"I forgot how old you are. Are you 85 years old?"
Two squeezes.
"Are you older than 85?"
Two squeezes.
"Are you older than 80?"
Two squeezes.
"Are you older than 70?"
Two squeezes.
"Are you older than 60?"
Two squeezes.
"Are you older than 50?"
One squeeze.
"Are you older than 55?"
Two squeezes.

That day, she was 52.
And at that moment, she believed I was 12.

I asked, "Do you have a daughter?"
One squeeze.
"Is she in school?"
One squeeze.
"Do her friends come over to the house?"
One hard squeeze.
"Okay, so a lot of kids come over?"
She nodded.
"Do you serve them chips and pop?"
One squeeze.
"Do boys come over?"
Two squeezes.

The message was clear: yes to friends; no to boys.

The *How Old Are You Today?* game hadn't disappeared, it had evolved. And so did we.

But the time for learning had passed. She couldn't tell new stories anymore.
Now, I asked the questions I already knew the answers to—because it gave us a way to stay connected.

The questions got smaller. More specific. But they still mattered.
We played this way until the end.

We played the game—one squeeze at a time—until there was nothing left to say.

Chapter 32
One More Day

Mom was resting—20 days shy of her 100th birthday. She slept quietly, dressed and lying atop the blanket, a faint smile on her face. She didn't wake up when I entered the room.

I sat beside her for hours. It was a monologue—I spoke about anything. I needed noise to fill the silence. I talked about travel updates, work, the dogs, random memories, whatever came to mind.

I couldn't sit still. So, I cleaned—anything to keep my hands and mind busy. I swept floors, organized her sock drawer, arranged mementos, straightened pictures, coordinated outfits, and bagged old clothes.

It was a ritual. A final act of care.

In the back of the closet, under scarves and old bags, I found her navy blue shoes with rainbows. Mom loved silly shoes—I used to make fun of hers. And here they were—waiting.

I wiped them slowly, carefully—like I was preparing her for the next step. Then I placed them by the bed.

Her peace said she was close to the end. Still warm. Still here.

I knelt beside her, holding her warm, bony fingers in mine. I memorized her hand: every line, every bend, every crease I'd never want to forget. I took a breath. I laid my head on her chest and listened. One more breath. One more moment of aliveness.

"Mom, you have lived a long and beautiful life. Almost 100 years—that's quite an achievement. These last years have been some of the best in my life. You taught me so much—about you, about me. You shared your stories. You brought me fully into your memories. Dementia has been a gift that healed us both. Caring for you was a blessing.

I know you're holding on for me. But it's time to go now—to be with Dad, your sisters and brothers, your mother and father. It's time to live a happy life on the other side. Just imagine—you can play gin rummy all day, every day.

Mom, I will miss and love you every day.
You've been the best mom.
I will be OK."

I stood, squeezed her hand, kissed her cheek, stroked her head. At the door, I turned for one more look. We were complete. And in love.

I whispered goodbye, soft as breath.

Chapter 33
The Morning After

That was the last time I saw my mom alive.

That night, I dreamed of her.

My phone rang—I thought it was part of the dream.
Then came the 4:00am call:
"Your mom passed during the night."

I've always believed the dream call was the moment she crossed over.

My mind went blank. My body went numb. I grabbed whatever clothes were closest and drove to the nursing home with nothing—no license, no money, nothing to identify me as me.

I entered her room. She looked the same as the day before—peaceful, asleep. But this time, it was forever.

The aide had dressed her, anticipating my arrival. She was wearing her favorite shoes—navy blue covered with rainbows—ready for her next destination.

The room was silent, holding her scent and presence, the heat just beginning to fade. I touched her hand—cold now—and I knew it was real.

The funeral director arrived with quiet dignity. He asked if there was anything I wanted to say before he took her out of her room.

"We have said everything to each other. We are complete, there is nothing more to say."

But as they wheeled her out, I followed and whispered, "I love you."

Then I returned to the room, alone. I sat on the bed, knowing this was the last time I would visit this room and nursing home. I had spent so much time in this space—and in the blink of an eye, my reason for visiting was gone. No tears. Just numb.

I gathered what remained: a small photograph, the painting that had watched over her—and me—for a lifetime. I took them with me. The last things left. The last things I carried.

I stopped for coffee, trying to settle my nerves. That's when it hit me, no wallet, no money. Nothing. I was unprepared—for this and for what was to come. I stood there, empty. The tears came fast. Rooted to the spot. People looked but left me alone. Somehow, they sensed it wasn't the time for words.

I went home and sat in silence.

Chapter 34
Still Talking

The silence after her passing was deafening—until it wasn't.

People were concerned. They'd heard my story and knew how close Mom and I had been.

After she passed, I kept saying aloud—sometimes in the car, sometimes in the shower—
"Mom, just send me a sign. Let me know you made it to the other side."

No answer.
Until there was.

A friend showed up with a big box of food to keep me going that week.

The box was labeled with the name of a company I hadn't thought about in years.

"Who brought this?" I asked.

My friend said, "I did."

"Where did you get the box?"

She shrugged. "Found it in my garage."

And then I laughed. Looked up and said,

"Thank you, Mom."

In high school, I'd dated someone whose family owned that company. We didn't last. For the rest of my life Mom reminded me, "You should have married that boy."

That box was no accident. That was her. Her humor. Her meddling. Her love, cloaked in packaging tape.

"Mom, got it. You're watching over me, sending signals, giving advice—and keeping your lifelong streak of tormenting me alive."

And honestly? I hope so.

I told the story, and everyone laughed. Because it was so her. And from that moment on, I knew she was close. We talk all the time.

It's not mystical.
It's not spooky.
It's just part of the relationship that never ended.

One of the most precious gifts my mom gave me in adulthood was the gift of her dementia.

Yes. A gift.

It slowed us down. It made room for patience, for small things, for shared memories that floated between past and present.

We didn't lose each other in that space—we found each other.

Chapter 35
Stories from Others

I owe my restored and loving relationship with my Mom to dementia and the *How Old Are You Today?* game. It gave me hope, peace, and a process to manage the twists and turns of the disease.

Whenever I was filled with fear or in a situation I didn't know how to handle, I would play the game. It calmed me, filled me with joy, and gave me stories to last a lifetime.

I often wondered if the magic of the game was meant only for Mom and me. So, I shared it with others. Here are their stories.

If you want to see how the Art and Rules appear inside these stories, flip back. You'll recognize them.

Make Your Bed

On a cross-country flight, I sat next to a young woman who worked in assisted living. We swapped dementia stories for hours.

She told me about a patient in her 70s who was labeled "difficult." She would rip apart the freshly made beds, sometimes three or four times in a row, and say, "Not good enough." The aides dreaded going to her room.

I told her about my mom and the *How Old Are You Today?* game. I urged her to try it—to find out how old the patient believed she was, and what her life looked like then.

A few weeks later, she messaged me. "Wow," she wrote.

The patient believed she was in her 40s. In her mind, she was back at work as a hotel housekeeping supervisor, in uniform, training new staff to clean and inspect rooms. No one passed unless they made the bed just right—often four or five times.

Once the aides understood where she was in her memory, everything changed.

She wasn't being difficult. She was doing her job — just like she always had.

Here, the caregivers protected her dignity. They adapted to her memory, matched her pace, and let her lead, inside the world she was in.

My Heart Hurts

I met a business acquaintance for coffee one afternoon. He looked exhausted, like he hadn't slept in days. I asked if he was okay.

He shook his head. "No. My father's in his 80s. He says he's in constant pain, but we've taken him to five doctors. They've run every test—they can't find anything wrong."

I told him about my mom and the founding of the *How Old Are You Today?* game. I mentioned that even though she was in her 90s, some days she thought she was in her 60s or 40s or 70s—and her body responded accordingly. Some days she looked younger; other days, she appeared older.

I asked, "How old do you think your father thinks he is?"

He paused. "I don't know."

Then I asked if he'd be willing to try the game with his father. He said yes.

I grabbed a napkin, wrote down the script, walked him through the questions, and explained how to ask them. He took a breath and said, "Okay. I'll try it."

A few days later, he called. "Are you a witch?"

I laughed. "Some people might say yes. What happened?"

"I played the game. He thinks he's 55."

At that time in his life, he'd had serious heart trouble—real pain, real fear.

Decades later, his mind had hit rewind, and his body was responding like it was in crisis all over again.

He wasn't imagining it. He was reliving it.

That's what dementia does.
It doesn't just remember.
It replays.
And the pain is just as real the second time.

Here, the son stayed curious. He didn't dismiss or try to fix it; he asked, listened, and let his father's experience be real.
He practiced emotional presence, even in the discomfort, and let go of what he wanted to hear—so he could hear what was true for his father.

Ring Me Up

An aide in Mom's nursing home shared a story. At the center of the floor was a circular station with computers where staff could observe the comings and goings of patients and visitors.

A woman would stand silently in front of the desk, just staring.

"It's weird," the aide said. "She never says anything, just stands there like she's waiting for something. It's unsettling."

I asked, "Do you have any idea what she's thinking?"

The aide shook her head. "No."

I told her about my mom and the game I'd developed—something that might help unlock a memory and provide an explanation for the woman's behavior.

If she was willing to try it, I walked her through the questions to ask.

The aide was skeptical but said she'd give it a shot.

A few weeks later, I ran into her in the hallway.

"You won't believe this," she said. "That woman I told you about—she thinks she's in her 50s. She loved shopping and believed I was a cashier. She was standing at a register, ready to check out."

She grinned. "So, I played along. I said, 'Next,' or 'May I help you?' She'd hand me her purchases, and I'd ring them up. Sometimes she had a real purse—real money. I'd give her back change and a smile. That's all she wanted: a finished transaction."

Here, the aide stayed curious. She adapted, matched the woman's pace, and let the moment unfold without judgment. She shifted from confusion to connection— all by meeting the woman inside her own story.

Your Story

Try the *How Old Are You Today?* game—not once, not twice, but over and over again.
It's not a magic trick.
It's a tool.
A way in.
A way through.
A way to connect.

This game gave me moments I never could've imagined.

I never would've known that my mom slept in a yellow room, wore gloves to work, was shy around boys, or feared for my life every day when I was a baby.
These weren't just memories; they were pieces of her life I had never known.

In the nine years I walked this path with Mom and dementia, I learned more about her—and about myself —than in all the decades before.

The words I heard in the closet—be quiet, watch, listen, travel—became the throughline. They shaped the art, guided the rules, and stayed with me through every story, every visit, every moment that came after.

Her dementia became one of the greatest gifts of my life.

I witnessed love.
I received it.
I returned it.

And when our time ended, I left with stories—and peace in my heart.

That's what I hope for you.

I hope you ask the questions.
I hope you hear the answers.
And I hope—one day—you'll look back and realize this journey gave you something you never saw coming: connection, clarity, and the chance to truly know someone you love in a way that transforms your lives.

About the Author

Glenna Hecht is a sought-after speaker, two-time author, consultant, and daughter who fought to stay connected when dementia tried to erase her mother.

Glenna has always been fascinated by how human connections can transform outcomes, whether caring for people in a company or caring for a loved one. For the past 15 years, she has led her own firm, Humanistic Consulting, delivering leadership development, training, and HR expertise to organizations across the country. She has worked with more than 70,000 employees, but her most personal and life-changing role was as a caregiver.

Glenna is committed to non-profit service, volunteers at Dallas theaters, and created the GJ Hecht Scholarship for Women who Make a Difference. Through her business, she donates proceeds to 13 global charities—because for her, making an impact means giving back. An Indiana University graduate with a degree in Communications and a minor in Business and Opera— yes, she sings—Glenna brings humor, energy, and authenticity to every stage and every page.

She lives in Dallas, Texas, with her loyal old dog, Louie, where she continues to write, speak, and support causes close to her heart.

www.ingramcontent.com/pod-product-compliance
Lightning Source LLC
Chambersburg PA
CBHW060425130626
46555CB00005B/2223